Born in 1918, James Joll was educated at Winchester
College and New College, Oxford. After army service
during the war, he was elected Fellow and Tutor of New
College, Oxford, in 1947, and from 1951 to 1967 was
Fellow and Sub-Warden of St Antony's College, Oxford.
Since 1967 he has held the Stevenson Chair of International
History in the University of London. His previous
publications include *The Second International 1889-1914*
(1955); *Intellectuals in Politics* (1960); *The Anarchists* (1964);
and *Europe Since 1870* (1973).

Modern Masters

Gramsci

James Joll

Fontana/Collins

First published in Fontana Paperbacks 1977
Second impression August 1979

Copyright © James Joll 1977

Made and printed in Great Britain by
William Collins Sons & Co. Ltd, Glasgow

Contents

Introduction

I

The end of capitalist society so confidently predicted by
Marx and Engels when they were writing the *Communist
Manifesto* in 1847 has still not come about. In the reces-
sion of the 1870s, in 1918 – 19, in the world economic
crisis of the early 1930s, at the end of the Second World
War, and most recently in 1973, many people prophesied
that the crisis of capitalism was at hand and that the
bourgeois economic and social order was about to collapse. The survival of capitalism in much of the world –
and especially in those countries which are industrially
most advanced – has posed to Marxist thinkers the problem of explaining the continuation of capitalism long after
it should have moved on from its highest phase into obliv-
ion. Most Marxist theorists have never succeeded in giving
an adequate answer, and one of the reasons why Antonio
Gramsci has assumed an importance which one might not
have expected, given his own political failure and the
fragmentary and difficult nature of much of his writings,
is that he suggested both reasons for the strength of
liberalism and capitalism and ways in which a revolutionary movement might gain ground even when the old
regime still seems firmly established in power.

'Who has *really* attempted to follow up the explorations
of Marx and Engels?' the contemporary French Marxist
Louis Althusser has written, 'I can only think of Gramsci.'[1]
The aspect of Gramsci's thought to which Althusser was
especially referring was his concern with the relation of
the superstructure of society to the underlying economic
forces which, according to Marx and Engels, determine it.
Gramsci rejected the crude dialectical materialism which
he thought was represented by the Bolshevik theorist

Bukharin, and he attempted to reformulate the doctrine of historical materialism in such a way as to allow room both for the influence of ideas on history and for the impact of the individual human will. This emphasis on intellectual and cultural influences rather than on purely economic ones enabled Gramsci to develop his doctrine of 'hegemony' – one of the concepts with which he is most associated in the minds of many people today – which goes part of the way to explain how a particular social and economic system maintains its hold and retains its support. Gramsci saw, in a way that few other Marxists have done, that the rule of one class over another does not depend on economic or physical power alone but rather on persuading the ruled to accept the system of beliefs of the ruling class and to share their social, cultural and moral values.

It is this emphasis on the cultural aspect of social relations which contributes to giving Gramsci a distinctive place in Marxist philosophy. Other twentieth-century Marxists – Trotsky himself, for example – have had a lively interest in the relation of art to revolution; and an attempt to develop a Marxist theory of literature was a main preoccupation of another well-known contemporary of Gramsci, György Lukàcs. But problems of culture, education and philosophy were far more central to Gramsci's thought and action than they were for Trotsky, while he was far more directly involved in political practice and organization than Lukàcs ever was.

Because of Gramsci's insistence that political leadership must be based on cultural and moral ascendancy as well as on economic predominance, he was led to consider two other problems with which Marxists and others in the western world today are necessarily concerned. Gramsci – and this no doubt accounts for the enthusiasm with which his writings are regarded by many intellectuals in western Europe and elsewhere – regarded the intellectuals as playing a central role in the revolutionary process,

8

and he had learnt from his historical studies, which probably went deeper than those of any other leading Marxist except for Marx himself, the essential part which an intellectual élite, such as the priesthood in the medieval Catholic Church, plays in the maintenance of a social and political system. Because of the importance which he gave to the role of an élite in the maintenance of the stability of a regime as well as in making revolutionary changes, Gramsci was also concerned both in theory and practice with the role of the political party. Whereas Lenin in his construction of the Bolshevik Party had stressed the importance of the Communist Party's leadership of the masses and had believed that the Party embodied the true class-consciousness of the proletariat and could thus exercise a dictatorship in its name, Gramsci was concerned with the participation of the masses in the political decisions of the Party, and with giving the phrase 'the dictatorship of the proletariat' a different emphasis. Even if he never resolved the practical and theoretical problems involved in the dialectical tension between leaders and led, party and masses, his concern with the question has again contributed to his influence on people who have been shocked by the tyranny to which, under Stalin, Lenin's conception of the Party had led.

Faced with what was done by Stalin and his successors in the name of Marx and Lenin, many Marxists in western Europe have tried to find an alternative Marxist tradition to which to return. They have seized eagerly on Marx's early works as suggesting another Marx whose humanism and links with the idealist tradition of Hegel had not yet been overlaid by the grim economic determinism of his later writings. They have turned to Rosa Luxemburg with her insistence on the need for spontaneous revolutionary action by the masses, or to those Marxist writers of the 1920s, such as Karl Korsch, who preached the need for decentralization of the revolutionary movement and for basing it on factory councils in which all workers would participate. They have looked further afield to China and have produced an idealized version of Mao Tse-tung's teachings which often bears very little relation to the practices of contemporary China. They have tried to create a systematic ideology out of Trotsky's writings, and by emphasizing his criticisms of Stalin's bureaucracy have tried to imply that somehow he was a more humane revolutionary than the other Bolshevik leaders. In this context, the writings of Gramsci have had much to offer. His attack on the cruder forms of historical materialism, his awareness of the complexity of history and of the importance of cultural factors in contributing to historical change, his attempts, in the Factory Council Movement in Turin in 1919 – 20, to find a new form of revolutionary organization which would combine effective leadership with real participation by the rank and file, have all been cited to show how the doctrines of Marx and Lenin might be used in ways different from those followed by Stalin.

Moreover, the fact that Gramsci was one of the founders of the Italian Communist Party and that, in the forty years since his death, he has been repeatedly, if sometimes contradictorily, quoted in support of the successive lines and current policies of the most important Communist party in the West, has also suggested that his writings might provide the answer to the problem of how a mass Communist party should operate in a non-Communist political and economic system. There are peculiar problems for a revolutionary party operating under a democratic constitution. If it is to attract and retain mass suport it must advance a political programme which will offer some immediate tangible gains to its supporters as well as the eventual prospect of a new society, and it must be able to link the day-to-day party activities with the hope of ultimate revolutionary success. Many of Gramsci's most important concepts – the idea of 'hegemony' which explains how a class can establish its cultural and moral superiority independently of its direct political power, or his distinction between 'active' and 'passive' revolutions — do seem to suggest ways in which a Communist party might, as the Italian Party in the 1970s appears to be doing, expand its influence and increase its support even without actual control of the government. Gramsci not only suggested the possibility of a more humane and more diversified form of Marxism than that used to justify the bureaucratic dictatorship and cruelty of the Soviet regime; he has also given indications of how a Communist party in a liberal democratic state might actually hope to attain power.

If Gramsci's political experience in the early days of the Italian Communist Party gave him an insight into the problems of recruiting and organizing a mass political party, his years of enforced reflection on that experience, during the period in prison which ended his life, gave an historical and philosophical dimension to his thought unusual among active politicians, whether Marxist or otherwise. Marxists can find in his writings suggestions about political organization and political action which are still relevant; but non-Marxists can find in Gramsci's work not only many original ideas about the relation of the past to the present, of economic systems of ideology, but also about literature or about education. He offers a challenge to liberal intellectuals which they can understand in their own terms, so that for all his hostility towards the intellectual tradition of which he was a product, he seems to provide a possible bridge between Marxist and non-Marxist thought.

Moreover, unlike some Marxists, Gramsci was a very good writer. His early studies of literature and linguistics left their mark not only on his way of thinking and his intellectual preoccupations but also on his style. The pungency of his journalism, the subtlety and breadth of the Prison Notebooks and, above all, the vivid and moving personal record in the *Letters from Prison* of his sufferings and his intellectual effort to transcend them, give Gramsci a place in the history of literature in the twentieth century as well as in the history of political ideas and of international Communism. He is a writer who will continue to be read not only by people looking for new ways of applying Marxist theory to contemporary European society but also by anyone who is concerned with our historical origins or who wishes to gain new insights into the tragedies and the achievements of the twentieth century.

II

Antonio Gramsci was born in 1891. He died in 1937. Of his forty-six years, some ten were spent as a student and then as an active political journalist in Turin, five were spent as one of the leaders of the Italian Communist Party during the crucial period in which Mussolini was establishing the Fascist regime in Italy, and ten were spent in Fascist prisons, or in clinics where he was still kept under guard although he was a dying man. It was a life which, when it ended, seemed to have been one of suffering, defeat and failure. Yet within ten years of his death, with the emergence of the Italian Communist Party as one of the most important political forces in post-war Italy, the influence of his writing was considerable, and over the past thirty years he has gradually won an international reputation as one of the most interesting and important political thinkers of the twentieth century and as, in the view of many, the most important European Communist theorist since Lenin.

Thought and action were inseparable in his life. 'My entire intellectual formation was of a polemical nature,' he wrote in prison, 'so that it's impossible for me to think "disinterestedly" or to study for the sake of studying.'[2] Yet at the same time he was constantly concerned to analyse his own political actions and those of others in terms of a general theory of history and society, and the enforced inactivity of his years in prison was used, in so far as his rapidly worsening health and the restriction of his circumstances allowed, to set his active political experience within a wider historical and philosophical framework.

Thus, although Gramsci's life was decisively interrupted by his arrest and imprisonment, there is a remarkable continuity in his thinking. And although, as any practical politician must, he changed his mind and contradicted himself on a number of occasions, certain central themes and fundamental attitudes developed consistently throughout his career.

On the other hand, the circumstances of his life were such that he left no extended piece of theoretical writing. From October 1914, when Gramsci's first signed article appeared, until his arrest on 8 November 1926, his writing took the form of regular articles for the newspapers and reviews with which he was associated, day-to-day journalism and criticism, most of which is not more than a page or two in length. And in prison, when he was thinking on a larger scale, he was for much of the time physically too weak and too circumscribed by prison conditions to write more than a few consecutive pages. Moreover, while his journalism can be dated accurately (and most of it has been collected and republished), even if there are sometimes doubts about the attribution of unsigned articles, the thirty-two Prison Notebooks present considerable problems of dating and interpretation, though this task has been made much easier by the publication in 1975 of a complete scholarly edition.

These scholarly editorial problems have been complicated still further by the active political discussions which have surrounded the publication and interpretation of Gramsci's works. The leader of the Italian Communist Party from its re-emergence after the fall of Mussolini until his death in 1964 was Palmiro Togliatti, a close associate and friend of Gramsci from his student days, who

was naturally anxious to use Gramsci's writings to justify,
as indeed they often seemed to, the Party's day-to-day
tactics. But, although Gramsci had been a loyal follower
of the Communist International and had, for example,
even if with some hesitation, joined in the condemnation
of Trotsky, there was no doubt that much of his thinking,
especially in the Prison Notebooks, was wholly incompatible with the orthodox Stalinist line of the 1940s and
1950s. Gramsci had indeed, 'by a pleasing irony of History',
as E. J. Hobsbawm has remarked, 'been saved from Stalin
because Mussolini had put him behind bars'.[3] Togliatti, on
the other hand, had only survived his years of exile in
Moscow by developing a highly sensitive political awareness of what could or could not be said, and it was only
gradually that the official Italian Communist version of
Gramsci's thought began to reveal some of its true depth
and complexity.

Just because Gramsci has been used to justify the policies
of the contemporary Italian Communist Party, critics of
those policies, both on the Left and the Right, have also
been anxious to enlist his posthumous support. The interpretation and re-interpretation of Gramsci's writings has become a major intellectual industry in Italy. There is a
Centre of Gramsci Studies in Rome: congresses are held to
discuss his views: the list of books and articles about him
is enormous and is steadily growing. Outside Italy too his
work has been seized on as providing a guide to revolutionary political action in the present. And, as so often
happens when people feel that they can claim the credit
for discovering a little-known thinker, some of his inter-
preters have become intensely possessive of 'their' Gramsci
and resentfully critical of other people who write about
him.

Yet, for all the scattered, fragmentary and often difficult
nature of Gramsci's writings, he is a thinker who is interesting enough to bear many rival interpretations. He made
a real attempt both to interpret and to change the world

in which he lived. If he failed in the latter aim, he has suggested many new ways of looking at European history and at twentieth-century society, and in his life and especially in the stoical courage which inspired his philosophical achievement during the years of imprisonment and of fatal illness, he remains a true intellectual hero of our time.

PART ONE

1 Origins

Antonio Gramsci came from a very poor family in one of the poorest and most backward parts of Italy. He was born in Sardinia and lived there until, at the age of twenty, he won a scholarship to the University of Turin. His father came of a middle-class family and had crossed to Sardinia from the mainland on an appointment to a minor job in the bureaucracy, as a clerk in the office of the local registrar.[1] Antonio's mother was Sardinian, from a family of small peasants and minor officials. Gramsci came, that is to say, from a class whose destiny and political behaviour was to be a main preoccupation of his later political thinking – the rural, and especially the southern, petty bourgeoisie. But although the family began by being comparatively prosperous by Sardinian standards, they were struck by disaster when Gramsci was seven years old. The father was arrested on charges of embezzlement and was sentenced to five years imprisonment; and when he came out he had no job. The consequence was that Antonio Gramsci and his six brothers and sisters grew up in extremely difficult circumstances and deep financial insecurity. He left the village school at the age of eleven, and worked as an office boy in the local land registry until, three years later, his parents managed to send him to a secondary school, even though it was one whose teachers, as he later recalled, 'weren't worth a dry fig'.[2] From there he moved to a *liceo* in Cagliari, the capital of Sardinia, where he lived with an elder brother who was working there. In 1911 he managed to win a scholarship to the University of Turin. Another successful candidate from Sardinia, later to be his closest political associate, was Palmiro Togliatti.

Gramsci

It was a sign of Gramsci's own intense intellectual enthusiasm and ambition and of the sacrifices which his family – and especially his mother, a woman of exceptional character and some culture – were prepared to make to obtain for him any education at all that he had, in spite of hardship and the inadequacies of the Italian provincial education system, gone thus far by the time he was twenty. Perhaps, too, it is a sign of the respect for intellectual achievement which is to be found in even the most backward sections of Italian society. Gramsci's education was not only obtained at the cost of personal deprivation for himself and his family: it was also achieved in spite of bad health and of a deformity of his back which stunted his growth and left him a hunchback.

These experiences doubtless contributed to making the young Gramsci a revolutionary; and the Sardinia in which he grew up provided plenty of examples of peasant rebelliousness, often expressed in the form of banditry, as well as of industrial unrest among the coal miners in the south-west of the island. If Gramsci's own lot had been a hard one, that of many Sardinians was even harder. Once during a strike in Turin, Gramsci spoke to a conscript from Sardinia, one of the soldiers brought in to deal with the unrest in the city, who refused to believe that the workers on strike were poor people, and who told Gramsci 'I know poor people and how they are dressed.'[3] The situation of the poor in the countryside of southern Italy and the islands remained far worse than that of the industrial workers, and Gramsci never forgot it. One of the constant themes of his writing was the contrast between the city and the country, the dialectical interaction between them, and the political relations between the urban working class and the peasantry.

Gramsci's roots in Sardinia were deep, not only because of his early experience of the poverty and social injustice in the island but because he had come to respect the indigenous folk culture of a backward community. He was fascinated by the Sardinian dialect, by its traditional poems and stories and by its linguistic origins. He had early acquired an interest in the study of language, and this was increased by his academic philological work at the university, but this interest was always related to the social origins and background of the language and literature which he studied. The situation in Sardinia was, too, a constant reminder of how superficial the unification of Italy had been and of the extent to which a true unity of the various regions of Italy had still to be effected. Again and again in his later writings he turned back to the days of the *Risorgimento* and the formation of the Italian kingdom in order to understand the nature of the social conflicts with which the Italian state was confronted more than half a century later.

When Gramsci came to Turin for his scholarship examination in 1911, it was his first trip to the mainland of Italy and his first encounter with a modern industrial city. 'A short walk reduces me to fear and trembling,' he wrote to his family, 'after just avoiding being run down by innumerable cars and trams.'[4] But he soon came to feel the political excitement and the historical importance of the city:

It is a modern city in the most literal historical sense of the word. In it is precipitated all the medieval rubble which still disfigures bourgeois society in Italy: half measures have been abolished; the comfortable cushions which deaden too violent a shock in social conflicts have been sent off to the rag merchant through the rapid, almost compulsive creation of a flexible and combative proletarian organization. The integral conscious class struggle which is characteristic of history at this moment is in Turin already fully defined.[5]

If part of his nature remained that of the provincial Sardinian shocked by the luxury of the city and by the shallowness and lubricity of its entertainment — he was soon writing theatrical criticism, castigating the commercial theatre and discovering for himself the work of Ibsen and Pirandello – another part of him responded to the dynamic attraction of the great city.

This was an experience he shared with many intellectuals of his generation, who were excited by the prospects which the industrial revolution and the technological progress of the new century seemed to hold out, and by the possibility of turning Italy from a backward into a progressive society. Gramsci had much sympathy with the iconoclasm of the writers and artists of the Futurist movement, with their readiness to destroy the old culture in order to build a new one. The Futurists, he wrote, looking back on the movement in 1921, 'had a clear and well-defined conception that our age, the age of industry, of the great working-class city, of intense and tumultuous life, had to have new forms of art, of philosophy, of social habits, of language . . .'[6] He shared with them the belief that Italy needed to make a great leap forward into the mechanized world of the twentieth century. From Marx, some of whose works he seems already to have known as a schoolboy, he had learnt the necessity of industrialization as a preliminary to the proletarian revolution. As he wrote of Agnelli, the founder of the Fiat automobile works, the most important industry in Turin, and of his fellow industrialists:

> I have a profound admiration for these men. They are the dominating rulers of our time, the kings much stronger and more useful than the kings of other times as well as of our own. They are the people who uproot the ignorant, surly masses of the countryside from their quiet, passive somnolence and throw them into the glowing crucible of our civilization . . . Agnelli founds factories, and of necessity the workers become socialists.[7]

Much of Gramsci's later thought can only be understood against his own personal background – his Sardinian origins, his first-hand experience of extreme poverty, the shock of his confrontation with the city and with the industrial working class of Turin. But equally his ideas can also only be understood in the context of the intellectual climate of Italy on the eve of the First World War, and of the Italian Socialist Party with which Gramsci and his fellow students, notably Palmiro Togliatti and Angelo Tasca, soon became associated.

The dominant influence in Italian intellectual life then and for many years to come was that of the philosopher Benedetto Croce, who was born in 1866. In a series of books from 1893 onwards, when he published an essay on *History subsumed under the concept of Art*, Croce attacked the positivist faith in the methods of the natural sciences and preached the importance of a subjective and intuitive imaginative understanding in the appreciation both of historical change and of artistic creation. In the 1890s Croce had been through a period in which he had studied Marx deeply, and through his study of Marx he had been led back to an interest in the philosophy of Hegel. Behind both these thinkers, with their conception of history as an all-embracing process with its own laws of development, lay for Croce the figure of the great Italian thinker of the early eighteenth century, Giambattista Vico, like Croce himself a Neapolitan. Vico had not only seen history as the cyclical working out of immutable laws but had also believed that the study of history embraced the study of all aspects of human thought and human society. By the end of the nineteenth century he had come to be recognized as an important forerunner of all historicist ways of thinking; Croce edited his major work, *La Scienza Nuova*, and both Croce and Gramsci were much influenced by his ideas and his language.

Croce criticized both Hegel and Marx as well as learning from them. Where he had more in common with Hegel than with Marx was in his insistence that history was the history of the human spirit, and that it was the development of man's soul rather than of his material

21

conditions which provided the key to historical under-standing. On the other hand, Croce saw historical change as only comprehensible in terms of individuals and of concrete situations; he never lost his sense of the par-ticular in history, of the quite specific combination of fac-tors which conditioned the spirit of each age. He was a representative of a great liberal tradition, and shared with Hegel the belief that history was the history of free-dom, and that each successive stage in its development was marked by a further realization of man's potential for liberty. In Croce's own work, and especially in his later writings during the Fascist period, this combination of liberalism and faith in an undefined world spirit often led to a rather empty high-minded belief that somehow every-thing would turn out all right. To the young Italian intel-lectuals before 1914, however, Croce's philosophy gave a sense of meaning and of moral purpose to the study of history and an awareness of the continuous relevance of the past to the present. Above all, Croce's view of history embraced all human activity – art, economics, philosophy – so that to study history was to study the whole of life.

The young Gramsci, studying literature and linguistics at the University of Turin, was inevitably caught up in these ideas of Croce as well as those of the great nineteenth-century literary historian, Francesco de Sanctis, for whom the study of literature was firmly rooted in the study of society and of the history of ideas. These were influences which, even as he became increasingly committed to Marxist ideas, Gramsci never lost. Throughout his life he continued to conduct, so to speak, a dialogue with Croce, and it is significant that some of the most extended pieces of writing in the Prison Notebooks are devoted to a discus-sion of Croce's philosophy. What Gramsci learnt from Croce was a belief in history as the intellectual activity which dominated and embraced all others – morals, politics, art – and as the way of relating the past to the present and the present to the future. From Croce, too, he derived an awareness of the limitations of positivism and of the inadequacy, as his later criticism of Bukharin's writing on the subject was to show, of the cruder forms of historical materialism propagated by some contemporary Marxists, and he had a conception of culture which was far deeper than that of many of his fellow Socialists.

Nevertheless, he was at the same time deeply critical of Croce, not only because of Croce's criticisms of Marxism and his increasingly anti-Marxist position as the years went by, but also because Croce, as the intellectual spokesman of Italian, indeed of European Liberalism, was the philosopher of the liberal democratic order to which Gramsci, from his student days onwards, was becoming increasingly hostile. He disliked too Croce's refusal to accept that a philosophical position such as his must necessarily lead to political action. Croce's philosophy remained speculative – a self-styled philosophy of spirit. Marxism was, however, in Gramsci's terminology, 'the philosophy of praxis', a philosophy which found its justification in practical activity. Gramsci admired the breadth and grandeur of Croce's thought and what he called the Goethean aspect of Croce. During the First World War, when, as Gramsci wrote, 'so many intellectuals lost their heads and . . . denied their own past . . . Croce remained imperturbable in his serenity and in the affirmation of his faith that "metaphysically evil could not prevail and that history is rationality".' (QC p. 1216)[8] But this lofty detachment and sense of being above the struggle could also lead to a refusal to accept responsibility, to what Gramsci called *ponziopilatismo*, the attitude of Pontius Pilate.

Yet for all his criticism of Croce, the debt remained. Just as, to use a parallel Gramsci himself drew, Marx had turned the philosophy of Hegel upside down and used it for his own ends, so Gramsci would do the same with Croce. He stressed what the philosophies of Marx and of Croce had in common: 'It seems to me that as the "philosophy of praxis" was the translation of Hegelianism into historicist language, so the philosophy of Croce is to a very notable degree a re-translation into speculative language of the philosophy of praxis.' (QC pp. 1232-3) This speculative element was its weakness, but all the same the two systems were both attempts to deal with what Gramsci was coming to see as the fundamental problems of historical change and human development. 'We are all to some degree,' he wrote in a letter from prison, 'part of the movement of moral and intellectual reform which in Italy stemmed from Benedetto Croce, and whose first premiss was that modern man can and should live without the help of religion – I mean of course without revealed religion, positivist religion, mythological religion, or whatever brand one cares to name.'[9]

Above all, Croce had suggested aspects of historical change which were of great importance to Gramsci's own theory of revolution. 'Croce's thought,' he wrote in prison, 'must at least be appreciated as a valuable instrument, and so it can be said that he directed attention energetically to the facts of culture and thought in the development of history, to the function of the great intellectuals in the organic life of civil society and the State . . .' (QC p. 1235) Unfortunately, the respect was not mutual: when the first volumes of Gramsci's Prison Notebooks were published in the 1940s, Croce, then in his eighties and still a dominant figure on the Italian scene, dismissed them as 'roughly sketched and tentative ideas, self-questionings, conjectures and doubts often unfounded . . . (lacking) that power of synthetic thought which discriminates, builds and integrates into a whole'.[10] Yet, for all that, Croce's claim – characteristically having it both ways – that 'Gramsci was one of us' (*Gramsci era uno dei nostri*) remains true.

If Croce provided the historicist framework within which Gramsci was to carry out his adaptation of Marxist ideas to the circumstances of Italy in the twentieth century, there were many other intellectual influences acting on the young Sardinian student during his years at the University of Turin. This was a moment when several Italian social theorists were not only coming to terms with Marxism, but were also producing their own analyses of what was wrong with Italian Liberalism. Vilfredo Pareto and Gaetano Mosca were both criticizing parliamentary institutions, while Pareto was developing and writing about his theory of élites; and these were views which had to be taken into account by anyone, as Gramsci was later to do, concerning himself with the role and nature of the political party. The writings of the Frenchman, Georges Sorel, were being translated, read and discussed by young Italian intellectuals and political activists – including the socialist journalist Benito Mussolini, who became the editor of the Milan Socialist paper *Avanti!* in 1912, when Gramsci was starting to make his first contacts with the Socialist movement. While Gramsci was later to be critical of those syndicalist followers of Sorel who were more concerned with developing Utopian visions of workers' control than with the tasks of day-to-day organization, he admired in Sorel what he called 'the virtues of his two masters: the harsh logic of Marx and the passionate plebeian eloquence of Proudhon',[11] and he sympathized with Sorel's contempt for formal liberal democracy. Sorel, too, insisted that it was the working class alone which had the moral virtues necessary to rejuvenate society, and that to perform this mission it must have a faith in itself and in its purposes. Socialism for Sorel, as it was to be for Gramsci, was something all-embracing, a secular religion, and above all a new culture. 'The lower classes,' as Sorel had written, 'are not in fact condemned to live off the scraps which the upper classes abandon to them.'[12] Gramsci was always to insist on the specific contribution which the working class had to make both culturally and politically, and on the need for it to operate from its own base and its own roots. Gramsci also shared Sorel's admiration for the way in which the Roman Catholic Church had survived and maintained its influence for centuries, and believed that for Socialism to achieve a comparable success it too must be based on a faith which would influence every aspect of life of its adherents.

Any discussion of Gramsci's experiences as a student and of the influences which affected his later thought must face the problem of how much Marx he read at this time. Much of Marx had been translated into Italian in Marx's own lifetime, and by 1911, when Gramsci went to the University, Italian intellectuals, whether through the historical and philosophical discussions of Croce or the sociological theories of Pareto, were widely aware of the main ideas of Marx, while the Socialist thinker Antonio Labriola was one of the most interesting Marxist theorists outside Germany and a writer widely known to Italians in the generation after his death in 1904. The language and ideas of Marx were therefore by now becoming familiar to any young Italian intellectual. We know, too, that Gramsci attended a course of lectures on Marx in 1914 – 15 by Professor Annibale Pastore, who later recalled Gramsci as being 'very restless, without knowing how or why he had to break away' from the influence of Croce.[18] But it seems likely that it was only several years later, after his career as an active Socialist militant had begun, that Gramsci really became a thoroughgoing Marxist. By then he could read German, and if one is to judge by the references in the Prison Notebooks, when he was often citing from memory from texts which were not available to him in prison, the work which had especially influenced him was the Introduction to the *Critique of Political Economy*. For the purely economic theories of Marx he never seems to have had any great interest. What concerned him above all was the problem of the relations between the structure and the superstructure, and of the historical moment of transition from one society to another. He often referred to the passage in the *Critique of Political Economy* in which Marx wrote that a society never tackles any task before the necessary and sufficient conditions for its accomplishment are already visible and that no society dissolves itself and is replaced before it has developed all the forms of life which are implicit in its economic relationships. It was the visible signs of impending historical change which interested him, and, above all, the system of cultural and moral values which characterized each particular society.

For the young poor provincial student in Turin between 1911 and 1915, what was important was not just the exposure to a wide range of ideas and intellectual experiences, but also his first contacts with a militant Socialist organization and with the day-to-day problems of the urban proletariat. Gramsci, with a few of his fellow-students later to be prominent in the Italian Socialist and Communist movements, including Togliatti and Angelo Tasca, witnessed at first hand in the spring of 1913 a three-month-long strike in the automobile industry, while, back in Sardinia for the summer, Gramsci observed the parliamentary elections, the first since the extension of the franchise in 1911 and so the first in Italian history in which the peasants participated. 'It was this experience,' his friend Tasca later remembered, 'that finally made Gramsci into a Socialist.'[14]

2 The Socialist Party

In these years before and during the First World War, while Gramsci was a student and then a journalist in Turin, and was beginning to develop his ideas about society, philosophy and history, the Italian Socialist Party, to which he naturally gravitated, was at the start of a long series of internal crises to which Gramsci himself was later to contribute. Like most of the Socialist parties of Europe, the Italian party had been divided into a reformist wing, which believed that the party had a role to play in improving society and the lot of the worker within the existing economic and constitutional framework, and an orthodox Marxist group which believed that history was on their side and that they only had to wait, to increase their numbers, to improve their organization and develop the class-consciousness of their members till the inevitable triumph of the proletariat as predicted by Marx came about. In the case of Italy these divisions were complicated by divergent attitudes to nationalism and to the imperialist claims and ambitions of the Italian state. In 1911, for instance, the Italians had gone to war with Turkey in order to win the North African province of Libya: some of the Socialists had supported the war both on general patriotic grounds and because they believed that the acquisition of colonies would raise the standard of living of the Italian working class and provide an outlet for surplus population. As a result, there had been a split in the party. The same pattern was to be repeated in 1914 on the outbreak of the Great War, with a majority of Italian Socialists supporting Italian neutrality, but with some prominent members of the party, including Benito Mussolini, leading the campaign for Italian intervention on the side of Britain and France. Indeed, Gramsci, in his first signed published article in October 1914, showed some sympathy with Mussolini's positive attitude towards the war because it would be wrong for the proletariat to remain passive spectators in such a crisis. As he said at the head of an article several years later – and it remained true all his life – '*Odio gli indifferenti*' (I hate the indifferent).[1] (This youthful reaction to Mussolini's appeal for action was something which was often brought up against him in his later career.)

The Italian labour movement was further divided between the orthodox Marxists for whom the revolutionary struggle took a political form, who believed, that is to say, in winning power through elections and organizing a party to challenge the old regime on parliamentary ground, and the syndicalists who believed in direct action by means of strikes and who condemned political action as a trick which would simply substitute one set of bosses for another. In Italy, an anarchist influence was also still strong – the veteran anarchist Errico Malatesta was one of the leaders in the strike movement during the 'Red Week' of June 1914 which threatened to paralyse the country. The war increased the social tensions in Italy and consequently also the tensions within the labour movement. Gramsci's increasingly active involvement in Socialist politics in the period between 1914 and 1919 therefore inevitably involved him in the factional quarrels within the party and also, more important, in defining his own position as regards syndicalism, anarchism, the correct tactics for a revolutionary party, the nature of Italian nationalism and the Italian state, and, above all, the relation of an intellectual to the revolutionary movement.

For it was certainly as an intellectual that Gramsci was developing in these years. He was continuing his academic work – especially in philology and literature – in spite of ill-health and periods of nervous prostration, but he was also beginning to be active as a journalist and to be more and more involved with Socialist politics in Turin. His articles for the period 1915 – 18 give some idea of the range of his interests, both political and cultural, and of his intellectual curiosity and independence.

Most of Gramsci's earliest published writings appeared in a weekly with a circulation of about 1500, *Il Grido del Popolo*, and he was, like any journalist starting his career, contributing articles on a number of subjects – essays on general themes, literary and theatre criticism and, increasingly as the war went on and as he began writing for the Turin edition of the principal Socialist newspaper *Avanti!*, political commentaries. He at once felt himself part of an international movement against war – the *Grido del Popolo* devoted a special issue to the great French critic of the policies of the belligerent governments, Romain Rolland. But he was also discovering an international literary world. He realized the powerful social influence which literature could exercise and especially the potential effect of the theatre. Ibsen and Pirandello were writers who could contribute to making a revolution. 'Pirandello', he wrote, 'is one of the shock-troops [*un ardito*] of the theatre. His plays are so many hand-grenades which burst in the brains of the spectators and produce the collapse of banality, ruins of sentiment and ideas.'[2] He was reading contemporary French writers and also discovering English literature, which he continued to enjoy all his life, even if some of his enthusiasms strike us as surprising today. 'Chesterton is a great artist whereas Conan Doyle is a mediocre writer',[3] he noted later, while in 1917 he published a translation of Kipling's *If* as 'a breviary for anti-clericals' (*Breviario per Laici*), 'an example of a morality unpolluted by Christianity which can be accepted by all men.'[4] Kipling indeed remained a favourite, and the *Jungle Book* a work to which Gramsci was to refer again and again later in his life.

The emphasis on cultural questions was perhaps in part the result of wartime conditions: even Gramsci's nonpolitical articles were heavily censored. But his early writing clearly reveals some of his main preoccupations. He believed, he said, in 'integral journalism'. It was impossible to isolate one aspect of human activity from another, and he thought, like Hegel, that political revolutions are preceded by a revolution in the spirit of the age. Revolutions are prepared by criticism and by the creation of a new cultural climate, and just as the French Revolution was preceded by the emergence of what Gramsci called a 'bourgeois spiritual International' so now the Socialist movement ought to be performing a similar function.[5] Gramsci was always insistent on the need to educate the workers in the widest possible sense. Such an educational movement, he wrote in 1920,

> tends to the creation of a new civilization, of new attitudes of life and thought, of new feeling: it does so by promoting among the class of manual and intellectual workers the spirit of enquiry in the philosophical and artistic field, in the field of historical investigation, in the field of the creation of new works of beauty and truth. A movement of this nature has as its first phase, a phase in which it is purely an instrument of struggle and a second phase in which its positive work of creation begins.[6]

But this new culture must not be dogmatic and one-sided. Although Gramsci could be as dogmatic and one-sided in his judgments as anybody, he was nevertheless willing to change his mind. While he was in prison he was shocked to learn, to take a minor example, that his young son wanted to read *Uncle Tom's Cabin*, 'a book written to affect the shopkeepers of North America many years ago'. Yet he re-read it and admitted that he found 'in the midst of so much conventionality and artificial propaganda, some quite robust features'.[7] 'The more the cultural life of an individual is broad and well-grounded,' he wrote in 1918, the closer his opinions are to the truth, they can be accepted by everyone: the more numerous the individuals of broad and well-grounded culture, the more popular opinions approach to truth – that is to say contain the truth in an immature and imperfect form which can be developed till it reaches maturity and perfection. It follows from this that the truth must never be presented in a dogmatic and absolute form, as if it were already mature and perfect. The truth, because it can be spread, must be adapted to the historical and cultural conditions of the social group in which we want it to be spread.[8]

Perhaps Gramsci never resolved the implicit conflict between the dogmatic certainty of the Marxists and the historical relativity and subjectivity of Croce, but at least he remained aware of it all his life.

In fact, one of Gramsci's main contributions to Marxism was his emphasis on the importance of culture and its relation to politics. It was this that led him never to dismiss ideas simply as products of economic forces. This is one aspect of Gramsci's discussion, to which we shall return later, of the relation between the structure and the superstructure, between the economic forces and the cultural, ideological and political movements to which they give rise. It was a relationship which Gramsci saw as a dialectical process in which each part influences the other, combining to form what Gramsci, in one of his most famous phrases, was to call the 'historic bloc'.

Gramsci's journalistic experience during the First World War was providing him with a store of literary and philosophical interests which were to condition his attitude to Marxism and which were to help him to carry on writing and thinking during his later years of imprisonment. He was also perfecting his style – sharp, sarcastic, but also more lucid than that of many Marxists and more precise than that of most Italian journalists. Above all, of course, it was in these years that he was gaining experience of practical politics as part of a journalistic team producing serious political newspapers in the face of all the difficulties caused by the war, reacting to the impact of the war or the workers of Turin and looking beyond Italy to the wider implications of the war for the International Socialist Movement. Gradually, from the end of 1915, in spite of his temperamental reserve, his physical weakness and his recurrent depression, Gramsci was beginning to make his mark among the Socialists of Turin. He quickly identified himself with the most radical elements and with those representatives of the minority of the International Socialist Movement who at Zimmerwald and Kienthal in 1915 and 1916 reaffirmed their opposition to the war and their faith in revolution. 'For us,' Gramsci wrote in November 1915 – and the language shows a characteristic mixture of Croce and Marx –

> the International is an act of the spirit, it is the consciousness which the proletarians of the whole world have . . .that they make up a unity, a bundle [*fascio*] of forces united in revolt although with a variety of national attitudes, which has as a common goal the substitution in the dynamism of history of the factor of production for the factor of capital, the violent irruption of the proletarian class, up to now without history or with a history which was only potential, into the vast movement which produces the life of the world.[9]

It was not surprising that Gramsci welcomed the Russian Revolution in February 1917. Perhaps what was more surprising was the speed with which he recognized the significance of the Bolshevik Party and of the ideas and personality of Lenin. Lenin, Gramsci wrote in July 1917, 'has been able to convert his thought into a force operating on history. The revolution is proceeding to its complete realization. The time is still far off in which even a relative respite will be possible. And life is always revolution.'[10] Lenin's writing was not known in Italy before 1917, and it was only gradually that texts by him began to reach

Italy from France and in the pages of the *Liberator*, the American review founded by Max Eastman. However, Lenin's name was already a symbol for the Torinese working class: when a deputation from the Petrograd Soviet visited Turin in August 1917 they were greeted with cries of 'Viva Lenin!' (which doubtless did not please them since they were Mensheviks and not Bolsheviks). After the success of the October Revolution, Lenin's pamphlets on *Imperialism* and *The State and Revolution* and other writings were, according to Togliatti,[11] becoming known in Italy and certainly by 1918 he was already an important influence on Gramsci.

Gramsci was fascinated by the Russian Revolution not only because it was a successful revolution, but also because he thought that it provided a pattern which the revolution in Italy might follow. Both Russia and Italy were countries in which the industrial revolution had come late and unevenly : both were countries with a large peasant population. The revolution of October 1917 seemed to demonstrate the possibility of by-passing the bourgeois revolution and going straight through to the revolution of the proletariat in a way which the orthodox Marxists had not thought possible. 'This is the revolution against Marx's Capital,' Gramsci wrote in January 1918.

> Facts have overcome ideologies . . . If the Bolsheviks deny some assertions in Capital they do not deny [Marx's] immanent, life-giving ideas . . . They are living Marx's thought, which does not die, which is the continuation of Italian and German idealistic philosophy which in Marx had become contaminated by positivistic and naturalistic incrustations. This philosophy always regards as the major factor in history not crude economic facts but man, men in society, men who interact with each other, who develop through these contacts . . . a collective social will, and understand economic facts and judge them or adapt them to their will until their will becomes the motive force of the economy, which moulds objective reality, which lives and moves

and becomes like volcanic matter in eruption which can be canalized at will.[12]

It is a passage which reflects Gramsci's excitement at the fragmentary news coming from Russia and his instinctive reaction in what were still Crocean terms; and it shows perhaps how superficial his Marxism still was. It is also a text which has often subsequently been held against Gramsci as proof of his 'idealism', his 'voluntarism', of his subjection to the ideas of Croce and Bergson. Certainly – largely under the influence of Lenin – he was over the next few years to become a much stricter Marxist, yet in his assessment of Lenin's own achievement, in his realization of the extent to which the Bolsheviks imposed their will on Russian society and the Russian economy, Gramsci's article remains a sign both of his understanding of what was happening in Russia and of his discontent, which was later to show itself in his criticism of Bukharin's *Theory of Historical Materialism*, with too crude an interpretation of the Marxist concept of dialectical materialism, and his sense, which he never lost, that purely economic explanations are rarely sufficient to account for historical phenomena.

3   The Factory Council Movement

The end of the war and the economic, social and political
disruption which followed, produced in Italy a prolonged
crisis which resulted in the rise to power of Mussolini and
the Fascists at the end of 1922. During these years, however, and especially in the 'Biennio Rosso', the Two Red
Years of 1919 – 20, it seemed to many participants and
observers that the chances of a successful Socialist revolution were very good. The trade unions increased their
membership from a quarter of a million in 1918 to two
million in 1920: in the parliamentary elections of November 1919, the Socialist Party gained a notable success. A
bitter struggle was engaged between workers and employers in all sections of Italian industry, while the
peasants and landless labourers were beginning to be
organized politically and to demand land reform. A wave
of strikes rocked the economic basis of the country and
filled the industrialists and middle classes with alarm, driv-
ing them into an alliance with Mussolini's new Fascist
movement which grew in strength during 1921 and 1922.
At the same time the liberal parliamentary system appeared increasingly unable to cope with the crisis, and
this breakdown seemed to provide the opportunity for
revolution.

It was in this atmosphere of tension and excitement that
Gramsci emerged from being a little-known young journalist to become one of the founders and leaders of the
Italian Communist Party, with a national, and indeed an
international reputation. Already in the late summer of
1917, the demonstrations in Turin against the war and
the violent protests against the shortages of food had
led to the arrest or mobilization of many of the local

leaders, and this placed Gramsci, who was unfit for military service, in a position of unusual responsibility. Then, eighteen months later, after the end of the war, Gramsci and his friends began to publish *L'Ordine Nuovo* (The New Order), which appeared as a 'weekly review of socialist culture' until January 1921, when it became – a sign, as we shall see of the changing climate of the Italian Socialist movement – a 'communist daily'.[1] *L'Ordine Nuovo* soon established itself as an influential paper with a substantial circulation in which general problems of Marxist ideology were discussed, the works of foreign writers translated and, above all, the day-to-day tactics of the Socialist Party leadership ruthlessly and relentlessly criticized. In its pages it is possible to follow week by week the shifting development of Gramsci's ideas as he was increasingly involved in practical political decisions and practical revolutionary activity. It was a period in which Gramsci was working out and trying to put into practice two of his most characteristic ideas – ideas which were in some sense incompatible, though each was to remain an important element in his thought. These were, first, the idea of basing the revolutionary movement on Factory Councils, and, second, the idea of the revolutionary party.

Turin was the most highly industrialized city in Italy and the number of workers in the automobile factories had increased enormously during the war. There was a strong trade union organization, and there were also well-established factory committees dating from before the war which had provided in less tense days a channel of communication between management and the shop-floor. With the example – though it was often misunderstood – of the role of the soviets in the Russian Revolution and the part played in the German revolution of 1918 – 19 by the workers' and soldiers' councils, it was natural that in the industrial conflicts in Turin in 1919 – 20 Factory Councils should seem an obvious form of organization for the

37

workers' movement to adopt. As Gramsci put it in June 1919: 'The socialist state already exists potentially in the institutions of social life characteristic of the exploited labouring class.'[2]

By the autumn of 1919, the Council movement had spread to many factories in Turin and elsewhere in Piedmont. For Gramsci they were not only to be the nucleus of a revolutionary movement, they were also to be a pattern for future society: 'The Factory Council is the model of the proletarian state. All the problems which are inherent in the organization of the proletarian state are inherent in the organization of the Councils.'[3] They were to be centres of education for the working class; and Socialist study centres at which Gramsci, Togliatti and Tasca taught were set up in connection with the Council movement. The Councils would provide, Gramsci hoped, a new way of organizing the ordinary workers which would preserve their spontaneity, enable them to participate in decisions and avoid the bureaucracy of the established trade union movement and what he thought of as the timidity of the Socialist Party leadership. 'The Party', he wrote,

> must acquire a precise and distinctive image: from being a petty-bourgeois parliamentary party it must become the party of the revolutionary proletariat which is struggling for the coming of a communist society by means of the workers' state, a homogeneous party with its own doctrine, its own tactics . . . a rigid and implacable discipline . . . The leadership, remaining always in contact with the sections, must become the motive force for proletarian action in all its developments. The sections must promote in all the factories, in the unions, in the co-operatives, in the barracks the formation of communist groups who incessantly spread among the masses the ideas and tactics of the Party, which will organize the creation of Factory Councils for the exercise of control over industrial and agricultural production which will put out the necessary propaganda to

achieve an organic conquest of the unions, the Chambers of Labour and the General Confederation of Labour, to become the elements of confidence to which the masses will delegate authority for the formation of political soviets and for the exercise of the dictatorship of the proletariat.[4]

It was certainly an ambitious and perhaps a contradictory programme, but it was an attempt, which Gramsci was to develop and to modify over the next few years, to solve the old problem of all revolutionary movements of how to reconcile freedom and authority, spontaneity and discipline.

Such a system of workers' democracy . . . would give shape and permanent discipline to the masses, it would be a magnificent school of political and administrative experience, it would involve the masses to the last man, accustoming them to tenacious perseverance, accustoming them to consider themselves as an army in the field, which needs cohesion if it is not to be destroyed and reduced to slavery.[5]

Gramsci was often to use such miltary metaphors, and to him the revolutionary movement had to be a disciplined, hierarchical, austere and dedicated force. Workers' democracy meant involving workers in accepting decisions taken by their leaders, the 'commissars' elected by the members of the Councils, drawing their authority from those who had elected them but subject to recall if they found themselves in a minority.[6] Implicit in the whole structure was the belief, which Gramsci was later to make a central part of his political philosophy, that it is possible through education and explanation, to persuade people to accept spontaneously decisions and ideas formulated by their leaders.

Gramsci's ideas about the role of the Factory Councils were based on the assumption that all the workers in a particular factory would be members of them. The Council movement, that is to say, would include both members of trade unions and unorganized labour, both supporters of the Socialist Party and people of other political beliefs. 'The class struggle in the present historical position of industrial capitalism,' Gramsci wrote in August 1919,

> is set in motion by a new type of proletarian organization, which is based on the factory and not on the craft, on the unit of production and not on the professional unions. This new type of organization, as it develops, grows and enriches itself with functions organized hierarchically, forms the scaffolding of the socialist state, the instrument of proletarian dictatorship in the field of industrial production.[7]

Such a proposal which would substitute a completely new system for the existing union structure was bound to meet the disapproval of the trade union leaders and especially those of the Metal-Workers Union, which was particularly powerful in the Turin automobile industry. Although compromises were reached from the summer of 1919 onwards, Gramsci's relations with the established union leaders were very bad. Moreover, since he was also repeatedly criticizing the leaders of the Socialist Party and did not hide his contempt for them, his relations with both branches of the labour leadership were growing steadily worse, though he was still hopeful that he would be able to win the support of the rank and file.

Given the history of industrial relations in Turin, its tradition of 'internal commissions' in the factories and the influence which the members of the *Ordine Nuovo* group had been able to establish, it is not surprising that in the summer and autumn of 1919 at a time of general industrial unrest and popular discontent, the Council movement had remarkable success, and it gave the impression that Turin really might become, as the phrase went, 'the Petrograd of the Italian Revolution'. However, elsewhere in Italy the example was not followed. The influence of Gramsci and his friends remained a local one, and the Turin experiment in industrial democracy in fact increased the divisions and disunity of the Italian labour movement. To the existing divisions between revolutionaries and reformists were now added divisions among the revolutionaries. While the Italian Socialist Party was expressing its admiration for Lenin, it was certainly not like the effective united revolutionary party which Lenin envisaged and which he had created in Russia.

One of the people who realized this and who was calling for the formation of a smaller, more compact and totally uncompromising revolutionary party was an engineer from Naples, Amadeo Bordiga, who already before the war had been advocating the creation of a truly revolutionary movement, which would not waste its time in theoretical discussion: at a congress of Young Socialists in 1912 he had denounced the influence of the intellectuals and the insistence on education and study which was to be so characteristic of Gramsci's attitude. 'The necessity of study,' Bordiga told the congress, 'is something proclaimed by a congress of school-teachers and not of socialists'.[8] By 1919 Bordiga was calling for the Socialist Party to abstain from parliamentary activity, get rid of the reformist wing and concentrate on revolutionary organization. For the next five or six years, he and Gramsci were to be the two rival poles between which the radical wing of the Italian Socialist Party, and the Italian Communist Party after its formal break with the Socialists in January 1921, were to oscillate.

The success in Turin of the Factory Council movement — *L'Ordine Nuovo* was selling over 5000 copies by the autumn of 1919 – obscured a number of ambiguities in the concept. We have already seen that Gramsci's realization of the need for leadership and discipline was not always in accordance with his insistence on the need for participation in revolutionary decisions by every member of the working class. And much of what Gramsci wrote about the Councils suggests that he saw them as a long-term revolutionary instrument, a means of educating the masses, of uniting the workers and creating the cohesion and confidence which would enable them to seize power. On the other hand events in Italy seemed to be moving towards a revolutionary situation in which some immediate action would be necessary and which would not leave time for the careful construction of a new-style revolutionary organization. There was an impressive general strike in June 1919 to express solidarity with the defeated revolutionaries in Hungary and the hard-pressed Bolsheviks in Russia. The Socialist Party at its congress in Bologna in October 1919, in addition to declaring its adherence to the Communist International, carried a resolution calling for the creation of soviets, although it was always uncertain what this would involve. For some, the soviets were to be a sort of corporatist substitute for the liberal parliamentary system, and for others a means of direct revolutionary action. This was certainly how Gramsci at certain moments envisaged them: 'The establishment of the councils is only valuable if it is conceived as the beginning of a revolutionary process. The exercise of control (in the factories) has a significance only if it is a stage in this process.'[9]

The trouble was that events were moving too fast for a revolutionary process to have time to develop. For this failure of the Socialists to control events, the leaders of the party, as Gramsci kept on pointing out, were partly to blame. The leading Socialists were using revolutionary language without really preparing for the revolution and without, it seems, really believing that the revolution was possible. At the same time, the industrialists, powerfully organized in the Confederation of Industry (*Confindustria*) were preparing to break the workers' movement and striving to win the support of the governmen in doing so. Gramsci described the situation in May 1920, as follows:

The Factory Council Movement

The present phase of the class struggle in Italy is the phase that precedes either the conquest of power by the revolutionary proletariat for the transition to new modes of distribution which will produce a recovery in production: or a tremendous reaction on the part of the governing class. No violence will be left untried in order to reduce the industrial and agricultural proletariat to slave labour: they will try inexorably to shatter the organism of political struggle of the working class (Socialist Party) and to incorporate the organs of economic resistance (trade unions and co-operatives) into the machinery of the bourgeois state.[10]

It was a reasonably true prediction of what the Fascists were to succeed in doing over the next five years.

In the spring of 1920, when Gramsci was making this comment, the confrontation had come to a head. The Turin industrialists refused to recognize the Factory Councils or to have dealings with them. In response a large number of workers went on strike. The employers retaliated with a lock-out, and the government sent a large number of troops to maintain order in the city. Meanwhile, in Milan the leaders of the Socialist Party were carrying on a somewhat abstract discussion about the role of soviets. As Gramsci complained, 'While in Turin the mass of workers were courageously defending the factory councils, in Milan they were chattering about projects and theoretical methods for the formation of councils as a form of political power to be won by the proletariat.'[11]

The defeat of the strikes in Turin in April 1920 was followed in September by renewed industrial unrest in many parts of Italy. In the industrial cities this took the form of the occupation of the factories: in parts of the South landless peasants occupied the estates of their absentee landlords. This time, after three weeks, during which there was widespread expectation of an imminent revolution and renewed fear of total economic collapse when the lira fell drastically on the foreign exchanges, there was a compromise; agreement was reached between the industrialists and the trade unions which was endorsed in a special referendum by a massive majority of the trade union membership. The settlement, for which the government had been largely responsible, was the last success of the liberal regime in Italy. It gave increased recognition to the unions in the structure of industry; it made economic concessions to their members. It was in fact an apparently successful attempt to reintegrate the organized labour movement into the structure of the state. This, indeed, was just what Gramsci had feared. At the outset of the occupation of the factories, on 20 September 1920, he had written, 'But the pure and simple occupation of the factories on the part of the working class, if it *indicates* the degree of weakness of capitalism and the degree of power of the proletariat does not produce in itself any new definitive position. *Power* remains in the hands of capital.'[12] From Gramsci's point of view in fact the year 1920 ended in disaster and disappointment. The industrialists of Turin had broken the Factory Council movement. Gramsci's isolation from most of the rest of the Socialist movement seemed complete. The occupation of the factories which, on Gramsci's general theories, should have been the culmination of a revolutionary wave, ended in the reinforcement of the reformist trade union leaders. Gramsci and his friends had failed to influence the Socialist movement outside Turin, and the power of the Factory Councils, which should have prepared the way for the next stage of the revolutionary process had been broken before the Councils could move on to the next phase. The ambiguity between the Councils as a school of revolution and the Councils as a means of immediate revolutionary action seemed to have been demonstrated.

Nevertheless, even if his direct influence had been limited, the years 1919 and 1920 had made Gramsci's name known outside the comparatively small circle in Turin in which he had spent the war years. He had become of

interest to the International Communist Movement too, because Lenin at the Comintern congress in July 1920 had,
to the dismay of the Italian delegation which was composed of both Right- and Left-wing critics of Gramsci and
contained no member of his group, singled out *L'Ordine
Nuovo*, and especially its article 'For a Renewal of the
Socialist Party' for special praise. Gramsci's advocacy of
the Factory Councils had involved him in thinking about
some of the fundamental problems of revolutionary
organization and the relation between the industrial
and political wings of the working-class movement, but
it had also alienated him from the leaders of the party
and of the unions. He and his friends in Turin were an
isolated minority; they were soon disagreeing among
themselves; and their disagreements reflected some of
the wider differences which were dividing and paralysing
the Italian Socialist Party. Gramsci, over the next months,
was to re-emerge as a national political figure in the complicated manoeuvres which ended in the splitting of the
Socialist Party at the Livorno congress in January 1921
and the creation of a separate Communist Party. These
experiences were to leave him a tougher and more ruthless
politician and a more skilled employer of Marxist dialectic,
and when necessary of Communist double-talk. But they
also contributed to his general development as a thinker
because they forced him to analyse what had gone wrong
in 1920. They also forced him to think more deeply about
the relationship between the workers and other groups,
notably the peasants. Above all it was over the next years
that he was working out his ideas about the revolutionary
party which remained central to his thinking.

4   The Communist Party

In January 1921 the Italian Socialist Party finally split after months of bitter debate on doctrine and tactics. A large minority of the delegates walked out of the party congress at Livorno to form the Communist Party of Italy. Gramsci was a delegate to the Livorno congress but did not play much part in the discussions, though he had continued to hope that the Communists might carry the majority with them and a split be avoided. (He was never an effective public speaker, and his influence was always exercised through his writings and among small groups of people rather than through a mass audience.) It was Amadeo Bordiga who took the lead in the split for which he had been working for the past two years, and it was he, with his rigid insistence on doctrinal purity, discipline and independence of all other groups, who dominated the Communist Party in its early stages. Gramsci was elected a member of the Central Committee of the Party, but not of the executive, and his main work was still his journalism. *L'Ordine Nuovo* became a daily and one of the Party's newspapers, and Gramsci continued as editor.

1921 and 1922 were difficult years for him both politically and personally. The Fascist Party was rapidly growing in strength: in many parts of North Italy their squads were engaged in what was almost a civil war against the Communists and Socialists (Gramsci used to be accompanied by a bodyguard when going from his lodgings to his editorial office); the liberal bourgeois state still appeared to be breaking down, but it no longer seemed that it would be replaced by a Socialist one. Although Gramsci never gave up hope of the revolution, he now realized that there was going to be a long period in which the workers' movement would be more concerned with preserving itself than with overthrowing the government.

On the personal level, too, this was a hard time. One of Gramsci's sisters died: one of his brothers became a Fascist. His health was very bad again; the strain of the campaign for the Factory Councils and the bitter disillusionment which followed had left him physically and nervously exhausted. However, he continued to work and to write and, although in private increasingly critical of Bordiga's sectarianism and his obstinate refusal to work with any other section of the labour movement in the defence against Fascism, he nevertheless accepted the Party line in public. Then, in May 1922, the Party decided that he should go to Moscow as its representative with the Comintern. It has sometimes been suggested that this was a move by Bordiga to get rid of an awkward critic and potential rival, but Bordiga was, for all his political intransigence, never petty in his personal relations. In fact, in spite of their bitter tactical and doctrinal disagreements Gramsci and Bordiga respected each other: 'Bordiga,' one of the early members of the Party recalled, 'felt and showed a lively anxiety for Gramsci's health and a profound admiration for his intelligence and knowledge. Gramsci admired in Bordiga the vigorous personality and his general ability and capacity for hard work, and he appreciated the positive side of the work he had done in very difficult conditions for the original construction and organization of the party.'[1] For a brief period in 1926-7 after they had both been arrested by the Fascists they were together in custody on the island of Ustica and on terms, it would seem, of affectionate friendship. It would, however, as Paolo Spriano, the historian of the Italian Communist Party, has suggested, not be out of character for the chiefs of the Comintern to want to have under their control an alternative leader for the Italian Party should they decided to dispense with Bordiga, as in fact they were to do two years later.

Gramsci was in Moscow during the critical months of 1922 which ended with Mussolini's appointment as Prime Minister in October, and the beginning of the Fascist era. During much of his time in Moscow, Gramsci was in a sanatorium recovering from a complete physical and nervous collapse. While there he met a family called Schucht – a mother and three daughters, one of whom, Giulia, was to become his wife and the mother of his two sons. In December 1923, Gramsci was sent by the Comintern to Vienna, and in May 1924 he returned to Italy. This was possible in spite of the Fascist persecution of the Communists because Gramsci was elected a deputy in the Italian parliament. Mussolini did not immediately abolish the parliamentary system though the Fascists were establishing control of the country and harassing their opponents, and for the moment members of parliament even from the opposition parties enjoyed a precarious immunity from arrest. On his return, Gramsci found himself the effective leader of the Communist Party, since, as we shall see, Bordiga was no longer prepared to follow the tactics laid down by the International.

From 1921 till his arrest late in 1926, therefore, Gramsci was deeply involved with the policies not only of the Italian Communist Party but also of the Communist International. His thinking, more than at any other period of his life, was concerned with the immediate problems of the Communist Party and its internal debates and with the constant and direct threat of Fascism. At the same time, since one of the basic reasons for the Communist Party's existence and its split with the Socialists was its acceptance of the authority of the Comintern, Gramsci's own ideas were having to conform to, or at least to adapt and interpret, the Party line at a moment when the International Communist Movement had to face the fact that the European revolution on which so many hopes had been based in 1919 and 1920 was not going to occur in the immediate future. Moreover at this time, during Lenin's fatal illness and after his death in 1924, the struggle for power inside the Russian Party was having repercussions throughout the whole International Communist Movement.

It was hardly a period when Gramsci's ideas about an ideal revolutionary party or the reorganization of the forces of production had much chance of being put into practice. However, it was at the same time a period when the maintenance of some sort of Party organization and its preservation in the face of the Fascist threat was necessarily a vital task. After the collapse of the Factory Council movement, Gramsci, realizing perhaps that the lack of a national Party organization had contributed to the failure of the Turin experience, began to develop ideas of a disciplined, hierarchically organized revolutionary party. Much of his writing in late 1920 and in 1921 was devoted to a repeated criticism of the Italian Socialist Party. Whatever the new party was going to be like, it was not going to be like that. He was particularly critical of the great tragic figure of Italian Socialism, Giacinto Menotti Serrati, who tried to perform the impossible task of keeping the Party united while at the same time accepting its adherence to the Third International which was insisting on the expulsion of the reformist Socialists; and Serratti claimed that the dictatorship of the proletariat would be exercised by the Socialist Party while at the same time realizing the difficulty and complexity of the situation in Italy:

> The revolution is not a magical act by this or that 'leader' . . . The Revolution is the sum of varied and diverse circumstances, of multiplex elements that together add up and lead to the solution in a given historical moment of a crisis that has stubborn and deep economic causes.[2]

Fundamentally, and in his more reflective moods, Gramsci would probably not have disagreed. But in the circumstances of 1920 – 1, he believed that this kind of refusal to act, just because things were so complex and just for the sake of preserving Party unity, could only lead to disaster. He too had written, some months before Serrati used the same phrase, 'the Revolution is not a magical act,' but he had gone on to say 'It is a dialectical progress of historical development,' and had called for the Factory Council to create a situation in which the workers 'no longer express their social will through the tumult and confusion of the parliamentary carnival but in the community of labour, face-to-face with the machine which enslaves them today and which tomorrow they will enslave.'[3]

For Gramsci, Serrati and the Socialist Party by now represented all that he disliked most in Italian life: in one of his most bitter articles he compared the Socialists to the figure of Pulcinella in the classical Italian *commedia dell'arte*:

> Pulcinella is the classic type of the Italian people, a good-for-nothing who doesn't give a damn for anything [*menefreghista*] and the socialist party in some of its attitudes is a good incarnation of this type. Pulcinella never takes anything seriously. Pulcinella has always fled from assuming full responsibility for his actions . . . They [the socialists] have taught that the class struggle is like a game where they are destined always to be right, because history sees to it that they are always right – a superior divinity which is so little influenced by men's actions as to make it like a mysterious fate, or better still like a clockwork merry-go-round which turns, turns, turns always in the same direction . . . But one day the game is dismantled, the merry-go-round is closed or runs backwards.[4]

Later, Gramsci thought it necessary to justify his attacks – and they often contained personal abuse of some of the leading Socialists – by saying at the second Congress of the Communist Party of Italy in 1922,

I thought that the carrying out of such a sharp polemic against the socialist chiefs was something necessary in the very interest of the working class. At the moment when reaction was prostrating the working class, it was at least necessary to succeed in persuading the masses that the responsibility for the defeat was not theirs, so that they should not lose confidence in themselves.[5]

By the time Serrati died in 1926 – having in the meanwhile joined the Communist Party – Gramsci was even prepared to pay a tribute to him.

Comrade Serrati was the most lofty and noble representative of the old generation of traditional Italian revolutionary socialism: he expressed whatever these earlier generations could express that was most generous and most disinterested . . . It is certain that Serrati was loved as no other head of a party has been in our country.[6]

In the years after the failure of the great protest movements of 1920, Gramsci's first reaction was to blame the Socialist Party leaders and to stress the need to correct the errors into which the masses were all too easily led:

Alas! Italian socialism, which for the great masses was formerly a spontaneous movement of revolt and awakening, a movement of liberation begun in a disorganized form, without too clear a consciousness of itself, tumultuous but full of warmth and full of every possibility for development, and full above all of a fruitful spirit of initiative and of a tenacious will to action, Italian socialism, in the mind of its theoreticians, in the mind of its chiefs and inspirers, had the bad luck to be associated with the driest, dustiest, most sterile philosophy of the nineteenth century, namely positivism.[7]

His renewed emphasis on the necessity of an élite party with leaders who had the will to act was partly the result of his disgust at the ambiguity of the Socialist leaders with their blind faith in the crudest forms of historical materialism, but it was also the result of a disgust – even if it was perhaps only a passing disgust – with the masses themselves. 'The leaders of the proletarian movement', he wrote just before the acceptance by the trade unions of the settlement with the employers which put an end to the occupation of the factories in September 1920,

> base themselves on the 'masses', that is they seek a pre-ventive consensus on action, moving to consultation in forms and at a time which they choose themselves. A revolu-tionary movement, on the other hand, bases itself only on the proletarian vanguard and must be led without preventive consultation, without the apparatus of representative assemblies. Revolution is like war: it must be minutely pre-pared by a workers' general staff, just as a war is prepared by the general staff of the army; assemblies can only ratify what has already happened, reward success and implacably punish failure. It is the duty of the proletarian vanguard to keep the revolutionary spirit permanently alive in the masses, to create the conditions in which the masses will be ready for action, in which the masses respond instantly to revolu-tionary orders. In the same way, nationalists and imperialists, with their frenetic preaching of patriotic unity and hatred against foreigners, try to create conditions in which the crowds will approve a war already contrived by the general staff of the army and the foreign office. No war would ever break out if the people were asked its permission first . . . In the same way, no revolutionary movement will be decreed by a workers' national assembly. The emancipation of the proletariat is not a labour of little account and little men; only he who can keep his heart strong and his will as sharp as a sword when the general disillusionment is at its worst can be regarded as a fighter for the working class, can be called a revolutionary.[8]

Gramsci's attempt to combine some form of industrial democracy with a strong party controlled by a dedicated élite meant that he not only criticized the Socialist Party for their inactivity and their compromises, but also had to distinguish himself sharply from the anarchists, a group with a considerable influence in the Italian labour movement at that time, some of whom had played an active part in the Factory Councils. For Gramsci, the anarchists were not only sectarians, priggishly aware of their own revolutionary purity – 'persuaded', as Gramsci put it, 'that they are the repositories of revealed revolutionary truth'[9] – they were also Utopians who failed to see that a successful revolutionary party must be based on a specifically proletarian class-consciousness. Such a class-consciousness was not something that would develop by itself, but would, according to Gramsci, have to be carefully fostered. The proletariat in existing industrial society was too disorganized, too wretched indeed, to understand its own true interests:

> To expect that a mass reduced to such conditions of physical and spiritual slavery could embody a spontaneous historical development, to expect that it would spontaneously begin and continue an act of revolutionary creation is an illusion of ideologists: to rely on the unique creative capacity of such a mass and not work systematically to organize a great army of disciplined and conscious militants, ready for every sacrifice, educated to put their slogans into practice simultaneously, ready to assume effective responsibility for the revolution, ready to be agents of the revolution – not to do this is a real betrayal of the working class and an unconscious counter-revolution in advance.[10]

Nor was the syndicalism of the Italian trade unions any better: 'Syndicalist theory', Gramsci had written in November 1919,

> . . . has been the theory of a particular form of organization, craft and industrial unions, and has been constructed on a basis of reality, certainly, but on a reality which had its

form moulded by the capitalist regime of free competition,
of private ownership of the labour force: it has therefore
constituted only a Utopia, a great castle of abstractions.[11]

The new revolutionary party must avoid the vague
optimism of the anarchists, and it must avoid the illusions
of the syndicalists who thought that, in a form of organization dictated by the structure of capitalist society, they
could still achieve revolutionary ends.

During his active years in the Communist Party, Gramsci
found himself in theoretical positions of some difficulty.
He believed that a working-class revolutionary party must
be based on a specific kind of class-consciousness. In both
its organization and in its moral values it must free itself
completely from the bourgeois world. On the other hand,
he was increasingly impatient with Bordiga's refusal to
make any agreement, even a tactical one, with any other
section of society. At the same time, while he still believed in the kind of participation in political decisions
which he thought had been achieved in the Factory Councils, he was insisting more and more on the necessity for
strong and clear leadership. Moreover while both he and
Bordiga shared Lenin's original concept of what a
revolutionary party should be like, they differed on what
this meant in the situation of Italy after 1922, and for
each of them in different ways it was becoming increasingly hard to reconcile the discipline demanded by the
Comintern with a realization of what was required in
Italy. To understand the debate between Gramsci and
Bordiga about the nature of the Communist Party and
the relationship of both of them to the Communist International, including their attitude to Trotsky, we must
understand how Gramsci analysed the nature of Fascism
and the ways to resist it.

5 Fascism

After more than fifty years, during which historians and political scientists have been able to analyse Fascism, to see its international aspect and to study the rise and fall of Fascist regimes in Germany and in other countries as well as in Italy, we have a far clearer idea of its nature than any observer in 1921 or 1922 could possibly have formed. It was only gradually that Gramsci realized both that Fascism was more than a very transitory phenomenon and that the structure of its support needed a sophisticated analysis if it was to conform both to the observable facts and to Marxist theory.

Fascism in Italy made its first appearance early in 1919, when Mussolini founded the Fascist movement, based on some of the elements which had in 1914–15 supported his campaign for Italian intervention in the war, and drawing its strength mainly from ex-servicemen who were disillusioned with civilian life, economically dissatisfied, and wounded in their national feelings because Italy had failed to win the territorial gains at the Peace Conference to which they felt that she was entitled. They tried to combine their extreme nationalism with a vague appeal for a new economic and social system, and they set themselves up as defenders of law and order against the threat of revolution: a typical example of their methods was the burning of the Milan offices of the Socialist newspaper *Avanti!* in April 1919. However, in the elections in the autumn of 1919 they were notably unsuccessful, and during the next two years Mussolini was systematically and effectively broadening the basis of his support. On the one hand, he aimed at becoming more respectable and winning financial and political backing from the industrialists, but at the same time he was organizing the Fascist squads into an efficient organization which succeeded in many areas of North Italy, often with the connivance if not the active support of the police and other government authorities, in terrorizing their opponents and exploiting the fear of revolution, especially in those provinces where the Socialists had been strong in local government. They thus made it increasingly hard for the Socialists to carry on their normal party and political activities. By the time that Gramsci left for Moscow in May 1922, the situation seemed to be one of incipient civil war.

Gramsci realized how brutally Italians were capable of acting towards each other:

> The class struggle has always assumed in Italy a very harsh character through the 'human' immaturity of some sections of the population. Cruelty and absence of sympathy are two characteristics peculiar to the Italian people, who pass from childish sentimentality to the most brutal and bloody ferocity, from passionate anger to the cold contemplation of the sufferings of others.[1]

The collapse of law and order was for him a sign of the failure of the liberal bourgeois state and a sign of its impending collapse: 'The destruction of the state, the end of law, the dissolution of society,' an unsigned article in *L'Ordine Nuovo* in May 1921, probably by Gramsci, states, 'in which terms we can sum up the political situation today, what are these if not the end of the bourgeoisie as a class capable of guaranteeing order, of creating and keeping alive a state?'[2] In these circumstances, each section of society found its own ways of trying to safeguard the conditions of its existence. The proletariat

> not finding in bourgeois legality, that is in the bourgeois state apparatus (the armed forces, the courts, the civil

service) the guarantees and elementary defence of its basic right to life, liberty, personal integrity and daily bread, is obliged to create its own legality, to create its own apparatus of resistance and defence.[3]

But this breakdown of the existing state and the end of the consensus on which liberal society rested had its consequences for the bourgeoisie too: and Fascism was one of them. 'Fascism is the illegal aspect of capitalist violence: the restoration of the state is the legalization of this violence.'[4] Fascism, Gramsci thought, was the only remaining way in which the capitalists could maintain their authority and preserve their economic system which had been profoundly strained by the war. 'Fascism is the attempt to resolve the problems of production and exchange with machine guns and revolvers.'[5]

However, although the Fascists served the purposes of the old ruling class, this was not the sole basis of their support. In a report to the Central Committee of the Communist Party in August 1924, Gramsci wrote: 'The characteristic fact of fascism consists in having succeeded in constituting a mass organization of the petty bourgeoisie. This is the first time in history that this has occurred.'[6] It was something he had already noted at the beginning of the Fascist upsurge in May 1921:

What is Italian fascism? It is the insurrection of the lowest stratum of the Italian bourgeoisie, the stratum of the lay-abouts [*fannulloni*], of the ignorant, of the adventurers to whom the war gave the illusion of being good for something and of necessarily counting for something, who have been carried forward by the state of political and moral decadence . . .[7]

The petty bourgeois, he was fond of saying, are like the *bandar-log*, the tribe of monkeys in Kipling's *Jungle Book*, rootless and destructive, a natural instrument for the counter-revolutionary intentions of the industrialists and landowners who make up the old ruling class. For this reason it was wrong, Gramsci believed, to talk of the Fascist seizure of power as a revolution, because the new regime had no class basis, and he also believed that, because it was not a true revolution, Fascism was basically no different from other forms of bourgeois rule. In order to preserve their social and economic position, the bourgeoisie were prepared to destroy the liberal state which they had built. 'There comes a point in history at which the bourgeoisie is obliged to repudiate what it itself has created. This point has been reached in Italy.'[8] If the Fascist seizure of power was just a symptom of the desperate situation of the bourgeoisie in their attempt to cling to power, their rule was still destined to give way to the revolution of the proletariat. At the very worst Fascism was not more than a transient phenomenon. As Gramsci put it later, 'The crisis consists precisely in the fact that the old is dying and the new cannot be born. In this interregnum the most varied phenomena appear.' (QC p. 311)[9] As he told the Central Committee of the Party in 1924, 'The general crisis of the capitalist system has not been arrested by the fascist regime . . . Fascism has simply slowed down the proletarian revolution, which after the fascist experience will be truly popular.'[10]

This last sentence gives the key to much of Gramsci's thinking in these years which aimed at finding new ways of making the revolution popular, and of winning mass support for a revolutionary party. He left for Moscow as the situation in Italy was worsening. Then, early in 1923, almost all of the Central Committee of the Communist Party of Italy, including Bordiga, were arrested, and although most of them were released later in the year it was a sign of how difficult any oppositional activity now was; from then on, the Party was forced bit by bit to transform itself into an underground movement. As Gramsci recovered from his breakdown in Moscow and then in Vienna, he was more optimistic than some of his colleagues who had remained in Italy. This was partly because, once he was over the worst of his illness, he was heartened by what he saw in Russia and by the direct contacts he had established with leaders of the International. 'The daily spectacle . . . of a people creating a new life, new morals, new relationships, new ways of thinking and of posing new problems made me more optimistic about our country and its future,'[11] he wrote from Vienna in 1923. This confidence had its disadvantages at a moment when he was personally lonely and easily tired. 'I receive many letters from Italian comrades,' he wrote to Giulia,

They want from me faith, enthusiasm, willpower, strength. They believe that I am an inexhaustible spring, that I am in a situation such that I cannot possibly fail to have all these gifts in such a quantity as to be able to distribute them generously.[12]

When he himself returned to Italy the situation of the Party was extremely difficult from many points of view, and the elections of April 1924 in which Gramsci himself was returned to parliament were in general a bad set-back for the Left and made the Fascists the largest party in parliament. Nevertheless, Gramsci retained his faith: 'Fascism has really created a permanently revolutionary situation as Tsarism had done in Russia.'[13] But he was worried by the fact that in the attempts to resist the growing encroachments of Fascism, the Communist Party remained a small and isolated group without mass support.

He analysed this weakness in terms of Bordiga's conception of the Party. Bordiga was determined to keep the Communists quite separate from any other anti-Fascist groups, since he refused to accept that there was any difference between the Fascists and any of the parties which had supported the former liberal regime. He agreed with Gramsci in considering the reformist Socialists as 'the left wing of the bourgeoisie', but Gramsci was coming to see that to win mass support in a period when the main issue seemed to be that of resistance to Fascism the Communists must seek to extend their appeal – certainly to the peasants and possibly even to sections of the liberal bourgeoisie.

To achieve this the Party would need to change its nature. Bordiga, Gramsci wrote while still in Vienna,

> does not conceive of the party as the result of a dialectical process in which the spontaneous movement of the revolutionary masses converges with the organizing and directing will of the centre, but only as something which develops in itself and which the masses will catch up with when the situation is propitious and when the crest of the revolutionary wave has reached its peak, or else when the party centre decides that it should start an offensive and go down to the masses to stimulate them and spur them to action.[14]

The Party, in Gramsci's view, must remain part of the working class; it must be prepared to follow the working class in its attitudes during the intermediate stages before the revolution rather than, as Bordiga believed, basing itself 'on looking forward to a moment in the future in which it will be its duty to steer the working class in the definitive assault for the conquest of power'.[15] The Party was the avant-garde of the proletariat, certainly, and it was the only organization capable of giving cohesion to all the forms which working-class activity took – the unions, the party press, the factory committees and so on : but to do this it must be in touch with, and command the confidence of, the proletarian masses, whether Party members or not.

This was not to say that the idea of revolution should be abandoned, or that the Party should seek mass support in the way the old Socialists had done, by compromise with the existing order. But if the revolution was to be successful, the revolutionary party had to be more than an isolated minority and had to have the strength of the masses behind it. If this were so, then the prospects were good, because the Fascist regime, even if it had delayed the revolution, was also preparing the ground for it. 'After the period of Fascist rule,' Gramsci said in a speech in Moscow – and it became one of the key doctrines for the Italian Communist Party after the fall of Mussolini twenty years later –

> we shall enter the period of decisive struggle for the proletariat, for the conquest of power. This period will arrive at a more or less distant time. It is difficult to say, to prophesy how the situation in Italy will develop. But we can assert that the decomposition of Fascism will mark the beginning of the decisive struggle for the conquest of power.[16]

At times, up to his arrest in November 1926, Gramsci saw signs that this moment might be near. He believed that there was a chance that the petty bourgeoisie alliance with whom he thought formed the basis of Fascist strength, would split and the support for Fascism be weakened. However, even if this happened, it was no time for compromising with the bourgeoisie just so as to restore the old pre-Fascist regime, even though Gramsci saw that the programme of liberty and order which the constitutional opposition supported would be preferable to the arbitrary violence of Fascism.

Gramsci was in any case convinced of the feebleness of the liberal opposition. In the summer of 1924 Mussolini faced a major crisis when it became clear that people in his immediate entourage had been responsible for the brutal murder of the reformist Socialist deputy, Matteotti. The opposition parties in parliament expressed their disgust by refusing to take part in its proceedings and withdrawing as a body to another meeting place on the

Aventine. However, they were unable to do more than make this gesture and found themselves powerless to overthrow Mussolini. In these circumstances, Gramsci, who was leader of the Communist parliamentary group which had initially joined the secession to the Aventine, decided that he and the other 18 Communist deputies should return to parliament and confront the Fascists directly. This was the occasion of Gramsci's only speech to parliament, a remarkable scene with an audience of hostile Fascists, including Mussolini himself, straining to catch every word uttered in his low voice and rapid delivery. The immediate issue was the introduction by the Fascist Government of a Bill outlawing the Freemasons. After a cool survey of Italian history since 1870 and of the working of the liberal state, Gramsci repeated his view that the Fascists had not made a revolution, because their regime was not based on a new class, but had merely changed the administrative personnel, and he attacked the hypocrisy of the law against the Freemasons: 'It isn't Freemasonry which concerns you! Freemasonry will become one wing of fascism. This law is intended for the workers and peasants who will understand this very well from the way in which they see this law applied.' He was increasingly interrupted by Mussolini and other leading Fascists and sometimes lost the thread of his argument. Finally after being recalled to the point, he ended bravely if a little lamely, 'The revolutionary movement will conquer fascism.'[17]

In 1920, after the failure of the Factory Council movement and the end of the occupation of the factories, Gramsci had believed that what was needed by a revolutionary party was stricter discipline and tighter organization. As, after 1922, the Fascists consolidated their power, and the Communist Party notably failed to attract mass support, he swung back again to the conception of a more broadly based party. There were two ways in which this mass support could be won: first by winning over those members of the working class who were still following the Socialists and second – for Gramsci sometimes even more important – by winning over the peasantry, a class with whom Gramsci had been particularly concerned ever since his youth in Sardinia.

In seeking to broaden the base of the Communist Party instead of, as Bordiga advocated, maintaining it as a small élite revolutionary group, Gramsci interpreted the situation in Italy in terms similar to those in which the Comintern leaders in Moscow were analysing the general situation in Europe. The result was that Bordiga was losing the support of the Comintern; and when Gramsci returned to Italy he was soon made Secretary-General of the Party. In the meantime, there had been a new attempt to win over Serrati and his Socialist supporters, since it had been decided that the policy of the united front of the working class was the correct way to oppose Fascism. It was a move which was only partially successful: true, the Italian Socialist Party split yet again, and Serrati and some of his followers joined the Communists, but the mass of the Socialists failed to come over, and the Communists were still a minority party.

By the time Gramsci returned to Italy, the International Communist Movement had suffered a number of setbacks, especially in Germany, where an attempt at a Communist rising in the autumn of 1923 had been a total disaster. At the same time, in Moscow itself, the breach between Trotsky and the other Party leaders was beginning to have repercussions throughout the whole Communist movement. When Gramsci replaced Bordiga as the effective leader of the Party, Bordiga remained an unyielding critic of the 'united front from below' and its implications as spelt out by Gramsci, who was now working for an alliance with all workers whatever their political allegiance, and, especially, with the peasants. Although Bordiga remained a member of the Party and of its Central Committee, as the crisis over Trotsky increased in intensity in Moscow, there were many people who saw similarities between Bordiga's proud and intransigent independence and that of Trotsky. For Gramsci, the danger of such a split in the Party was that it would result in the members losing confidence in the leadership. 'The attitude of Bordiga, like that of Trotsky,' he wrote, 'has disastrous repercussions; when a comrade of the value of Bordiga stands to one side [*si apparta*], a lack of confidence in the party is produced among the workers and this results in defeatism.'[18]

Gramsci was desperately anxious to turn the Party away from its recent feuds over relations with Serrati and the Socialists: the new Party newspaper was deliberately named *Unità*. Since he felt that, in the black atmosphere of Fascist repression, the Party was bound to rely on support from Russia, he was anxious that unity should be maintained on the international as well as the national level. He was therefore extremely worried about the divisions within the Russian Communist Party. He had some sympathy with Trotsky's criticism of the growing bureaucratization in Russia: but above all he was distressed at the implications of the Russian leadership tearing itself apart. 'You are today destroying your work,' he wrote to the Russian leaders in 1926 not long before his arrest. 'You are degrading the party and running the risk of destroying the directing role which the Communist Party of the Soviet Union had acquired under the impulse of Lenin.'[19] While he blamed the 'Left' – Trotsky and Bordiga – for these divisions, he believed at this critical moment unity to be essential. Once again he was caught in his perpetual dilemma between discipline and liberty and he did not despair of reconciling the two. There was, he believed, room for discussion and disagreement between groups within the Party as long as they did not lead to an open split. 'But unity and discipline in this case cannot be mechanical and enforced; they must be based on loyalty and conviction and not like an enemy detachment imprisoned and besieged which thinks of escape and of a surprise break out.'[20] Within a few weeks of his letter to the Russian Party, Gramsci was arrested and his active career as a political leader was over, so that, unlike his friend Togliatti who went to Moscow and survived the Stalinist period, or Tasca who, as an exile in Paris published Gramsci's letter to the Soviet leaders, and who, expelled from the Party, became one of its most bitter critics, Gramsci never had to face the tests and strains which Stalin imposed on the International Communist Movement.

6   The Lyons Theses and the Southern Question

In the two and a half years between Gramsci's return to Italy and his arrest, he had been involved in the practical problems of leading the Communist Party, of trying to widen the basis for its support, of adapting it to a clandestine existence, as the persecution of the Fascist Government increased. He had been worried by the divisions in the Soviet Party and had been concerned about the damage the breach with Trotsky might cause to the Italian and other parties in the International. Although his interpretation of the Comintern party line had brought him to the leadership in place of Bordiga, he was anxious that Bordiga should not be expelled from the Central Committee and that the unity of the Party should be maintained. His theoretical work in this period was therefore necessarily within the context of difficult and exacting day-to-day organizational and tactical problems. Nevertheless, there are two documents in which his general position in 1925 – 6 was made clear, but which also dealt with the major themes which were to preoccupy him during his time in prison. The first of these documents was the so-called Lyons Theses, in the drafting of which Gramsci played a large part and which were adopted by the Italian Communist Party at a congress held in January 1926 at Lyons in France, now that it was impossible for the party to hold such a meeting in Italy. The second was an essay, uncompleted at the time of Gramsci's arrest, 'Some considerations on the southern question' (*Alcuni temi della questione meridionale*).

The Lyons Theses and the discussion of them at the congress, at which Gramsci is said to have spoken for four hours and Bordiga for seven, mark both Gramsci's victory over Bordiga and his commitment to the line of the International. They also demonstrate the principles on which he had been reorganizing the Party over the previous two years. At the Lyons congress, Gramsci stressed, as always, that the Party must be part of the working class and not, as Bordiga maintained, an organ of the working-class movement separate from the masses whom it was intended to direct. He accepted the necessity of a united front from below, in which the Communists, because of their dedication and example, would be joined by the rank and file of the other working-class parties and groups, the more so now that the Social Democrats and Liberals had shown their inability to organize any effective resistance to Fascism. The Fascist experience had demonstrated that the revolutionary party of workers and peasants was the only possible alternative form of government to Fascism. Moreover, the unevenness of economic development in Italy meant, Gramsci believed, that capitalism might be more easily overthrown than in the other advanced industrial countries of western Europe. In order to produce a party which could survive both Fascist persecution and prepare the way for revolution, he agreed with the Comintern that 'bolshevization' of the Party was necessary: the Party was to be constructed on the basis of tightly organized cells, but for Gramsci these cells were to be the old Factory Councils adapted to changed circumstances.

The decisons of the Lyons congress were the high point of Gramsci's achievement as a practical political leader, and are a characteristic attempt to combine devotion to the line of the Communist International with a realization of the peculiar situation of Italy and to reconcile the participation of the rank and file with the preservation of Party discipline. The Lyons Theses are clear, too, about the role of intellectuals in the Party and the way in which the Party can attain 'hegemony' over other groups in society by its superior organization and superior understanding of the objective situation.

These were themes which Gramsci was in 1926 also developing in a more theoretical way in his essay on the southern question. Gramsci's early experience in Turin had convinced him that it was to the city that the country-side must look for its redemption. He had soon personally become identified with city life. As one of the most perceptive of his non-Socialist friends in Turin put it, 'he seemed to have come from the country to forget his traditions, to substitute for the diseased inheritance of Sardinian anachronism an intense and inexorable effort towards the modernity of the city dweller'.[1] But nevertheless for him town and country were indissolubly linked. Gramsci's concern with the relationship between the city and the countryside explains many of the key ideas of his mature political writing, both on the nature of what he called hegemony – the way in which a minority can impose its leadership and its values on a majority – and on the nature of the Italian state and of the basis on which its unity had been established during the *Risorgimento*, somewhat precariously, as he believed.

The urban working class could by its actions affect the conditions under which the peasants lived. They had, for instance, resisted the demands for a protective tariff which would have had disastrous consequences for the peasantry, turning over to inefficient grain production land which would serve other purposes better:

It is not paradoxical that a strike in Turin because of a threatened rise in the price of bread can serve also to rescue Sardinia and Calabria from the disastrous mania of cutting down trees to sow grain, in the mistaken confidence that high prices would at once increase the returns on land where trees alone can find nourishment in the water of the sub-soil and can become in a future economic arrangement the true and most profitable source of riches.[2]

When the Russian Revolution broke out, Gramsci had been quick to see that, even if Marxist theory demanded that the urban proletariat should be the vanguard of the revolution, it was the peasant masses who had provided the basic revolutionary upsurge and given the revolution most of its mass support. When therefore, from 1923 onwards, he became increasingly concerned with ways of providing the Italian Communist Party with a broader base than that envisaged by Bordiga, it was natural that he should see the answer to the problem in an alliance between the workers and peasants. But the peasant on his own – ignorant, poor, isolated – only felt an undirected discontent which it was important to control. His own revolutionary instincts if they were followed would only lead to disaster:

What does a poor peasant obtain by invading an uncultivated or badly cultivated piece of land? Without machines, without a house at his place of work, without credit to wait for the time of harvest, without co-operative institutions which will acquire the crop itself . . . and save him from the claws of the usurers, what can a poor peasant expect from seizing the land? It satisfies for the first moment his primitive greed for land; but at the next moment when he realizes that his own arms are not enough to break up the soil which only dynamite can break up, when he realizes that seeds are needed and fertilizers and tools, and thinks of the future series of days and nights to be spent on a piece of land without a house, without water, with malaria, the peasant realizes his own impotence, his isolation, his desperate condition and becomes a brigand and not a revolutionary, becomes an assassin of the 'gentry', not a fighter for 'workers' and peasants' ' communism.[8]

The only thing that could save the peasants and harness their instinctive feelings of revolt to a constructive purpose was to co-operate with the revolutionary workers of the towns. In Italian terms this meant an alliance between the industrial areas of the north and the backward and under-developed south. It was also a way of saving the unity of Italy: just as, according to Gramsci, the middle class had been the 'national' class in the *Risorgimento*, the historical instrument for the creation of Italian unity, so now the proletariat would be the 'national class', which would make that unity a social and economic reality. 'In Italy,' Gramsci wrote in 1925,

> the situation is revolutionary when the proletariat of the north is strong; if the proletariat of the north is weak, the peasants will reach agreement with the petty bourgeoisie, and equally the peasants of southern Italy represent an element of strength and a revolutionary impulse for the workers in the north. The northern workers and the southern peasants are the two formidable revolutionary forces . . . to which we should all turn our attention.[4]

The task was clearly not an easy one: for decades the peasantry had looked to the bourgeois intellectuals, the doctors and lawyers and pharmacists of the small towns, for their political leadership, or else, more important still, to the Church. If the Communists were to break the hold of these traditional centres of influence over the peasantry, they were not only going to have to organize the revolutionary elements among the peasants themselves, to establish Communist cells in the countryside, but they were also going to have to provide the intellectual leadership hitherto given by their bourgeois and clerical rivals.

Gramsci always admired the organization and propaganda of the Roman Catholic Church. He had followed with interest the rise and fall of the *Partito Popolare* between 1919 and 1922 – an attempt to organize a popular and progressive Catholic political party among the peasants of the south. If the Communist Party was to succeed in replacing Catholic influence among the peasants with its own doctrine, it would have to compete by providing not only an ideology of equal historical importance, but also its own equivalent of the priesthood, an intellectual class which could convince the peasants that they were linked to them and shared common roots, common goals and common aspirations. Gramsci's reflections on the need to win peasant support and on the relations between the north and the south of Italy brought him up against the problems which were to occupy him for the rest of his life: the role of the intellectuals in society, the nature of historical tradition and historical change, and the way in which the hegemony of a ruling group is exercised over the masses. When he was arrested in 1926, he was working on a substantial theoretical discussion of some of these problems and raising many of the topics with which he was to fill his prison notebooks over the next ten years. The experiences of practical politics in the Communist Party provided the basis of his theoretical thinking when the practice of politics was barred to him.

PART TWO

7 Prison

On 8 November 1926 Antonio Gramsci was arrested by
Mussolini's police on his way to parliament, which was
about to approve a law restoring the death penalty and
setting up a special court to try political offenders. He had
rejected suggestions that he should seek refuge abroad
and had been living a semi-clandestine life in Rome. His
wife Giulia had been with him for a few months, but had
already returned to Moscow with their elder son, Delio;
the younger son, Giuliano, was born soon after her arrival
in Russia and never saw his father.

At first Gramsci was sent to the island of Ustica, where
a number of political prisoners were detained, including
Bordiga, with whom Gramsci, on the best personal terms
with his old opponent, was soon organizing classes for
the other inmates. This comparatively easy existence did
not last long. After being moved from Ustica to Milan,
he was eventually brought to trial in Rome before the new
political court, the Special Tribunal for the Defence of the
State, together with some other leading Communists. At
the beginning of June 1928, he was sentenced to twenty
years' imprisonment. By the time he began his formal
sentence after eighteen months' imprisonment, Gramsci's
health had deteriorated seriously, and he was sent to a
special prison for unfit prisoners (though the medical
provisions seem to have been minimal) at Turi, near Bari in
the south of Italy. He remained there until 1933, when,
after a critical illness, his condition was so bad that,
partly as a result of an international campaign on his be-
half, he was allowed to be moved to a private clinic at
Formia, between Rome and Naples, though still behind
bars and under guard: he was later moved to another

clinic in Rome, under slightly better conditions, but his
health was now totally destroyed, and he died on 27
April 1937, just as the order for his provisional release
on the grounds of ill-health had been signed.

Mussolini is said to have demanded – and it was repeated
by the prosecutor at Gramsci's trial – 'We must prevent
this brain from functioning for twenty years.' This the
Fascists notably failed to do: but the difficulties they
placed in the way of Gramsci's expressing himself were at
first considerable. It was some time before he was allowed
writing materials in his cell: the number of letters he was
permitted was strictly rationed. Nevertheless, in spite of all
this he succeeded during his imprisonment in filling 33
notebooks (which take up some 2350 printed pages) with
his ideas on history, philosophy, politics and literature,
and in writing to his family long letters which give a
vivid picture of his life and sufferings in prison as well
as an idea of his intellectual preoccupations. Most of these
letters were addressed to his sister-in-law Tatiana, who remained in Italy and assumed the responsibility for giving
him such help as she could, by writing, by visiting him
and – often against his wishes – by trying every legal,
political and personal means to gain his release or at least
to obtain proper medical care for him. His letters to her
provided an outlet for his irritation and frustration as
well as for his hopes, his fears and his plans for reading and study. The fact that he was able to read widely
and to receive books and reviews, as far as the prison
authorities permitted – and they seem in some ways to
have been remarkably liberal once he had permission to
study and write – was mainly due to his friend Piero
Sraffa, who had settled in England and became a distinguished economist at Cambridge, and who opened an
account for Gramsci with a Milan bookseller.

Yet his isolation remained very great: he had virtually
no contact with his former political associates, most of
whom were in exile or themselves in prison. The evidence

of Gramsci's reaction to the crisis in the International after the disgrace of Trotsky is slender and sometimes obscure: and it is not really clear from the conflicting accounts of fellow-prisoners and one of his brothers what his attitude was to the great discussion, which split the Italian Communist Party in 1930, about whether the fall of Fascism would be immediately followed, as Gramsci had sometimes believed, by the revolution and the establishment of the dictatorship of the proletariat, or whether there would be, as he seems to have been thinking just before his arrest, a return to a liberal democracy first. Whereas during his active political career we often have to deduce Gramsci's ideas from his day-to-day tactical writing, the Prison Notebooks and the letters discuss general problems and abstract ideas without much reference to the practical political activity which was now denied to him.

Gramsci's enforced isolation was often painful. 'Boredom,' he wrote to his mother,

> is my worst enemy, although I read or write all day long; it's a special kind of boredom which doesn't spring from idleness . . . but from the lack of contact with the outside world. I don't know whether you've read the lives of saints and hermits; they were tormented by this special boredom, which they called the 'noonday devil' because towards midday they were seized . . . by a longing for change, to return to the world, to see people.[1]

But the lack of immediate contact with the outside world forced Gramsci to draw on his past political and journalistic activity and to combine it with his current reading so as to produce a whole series of reflections and essays based on a long historical perspective as well as on his own recent political experience.

He was dissatisfied with his journalism: 'In ten years of journalism,' he wrote to Tatiana,

I've produced enough material to fill fifteen or twenty volumes of four hundred pages each; but these pages were turned out every day and should have, I believe, been forgotten immediately afterwards.[2]

He was full of plans for a major philosophical or historical work:

> . . . One is research on the history of Italian intellectuals, their origins and groupings in relation to cultural currents, their various modes of thinking and so on . . . Do you remember that short superficial essay of mine about southern Italy and the importance of B. Croce? Well, I'd like to elaborate the thesis I only touched on then, from a disinterested point of view, *für ewig*. Second a study of comparative linguistics, nothing less! . . . Third a study of Pirandello and the transformation of theatrical taste in Italy that he represented and helped determine . . . Fourth an essay on feuilletons and popular taste in literature . . . How does all this strike you? Really, if you look closely at these four arguments, a common thread runs through them: the popular creative spirit, in its diverse phases of development, is equally present in each.[3]

Gramsci's failing health and the difficulties of work under prison conditions prevented him from completing any of these ambitious projects, but the themes were among those which occupied a central place in the reflections with which, over the next few years, he was to fill his Prison Notebooks.

8   Historical Materialism and the Dialectic

The framework of Gramsci's thinking was provided by his Marxism, or, as he called it in the Prison Notebooks, the Philosophy of Praxis. It was a phrase used partly to mislead the prison officials – just as he called Lenin Ilich, Trotsky Bronstein, and Stalin, in the rare references to him, Giuseppe Bessarione, (Joseph Vissarionovich) – but it accurately reflected his conception of what political philosophy should be. It should provide a method for the interpretation of the world so as to be a guide to action. But Gramsci's Marxism was a very personal one. He never entirely rejected the historicism of Croce; and many pages of the Notebooks were filled with a critical discussion of Croce's ideas. It is as if a perpetual dialogue between Lenin and Croce was being conducted within his mind, for he was equally deeply influenced by Lenin's theory and practice, and many of his concepts, such as that of 'hegemony' which was a central feature of his historical and political analysis were derived from Lenin. He once claimed that

> The position of *L'Ordine Nuovo* consisted essentially . . . in having translated the principles demanded by the doctrine and tactics of the Communist International into Italian historical language.[1]

And he continued to do this with Marxism in general, so that he is more aware of a historical dimension to Marxism and more conscious of its cultural implications than any other Marxist thinker. He believed that what had gone wrong with Marxism, with, he thought, disastrous effects on the ideology and practice of the Italian Socialist Party, was its association with positivism and with a crude and insensitive materialism.

His basic attitude of historical materialism – and a discussion of it leads on to a discussion of his views on history and historical change – is made clear in the passages in the Notebooks which he devotes to criticizing one of the key works of Soviet theoretical writing, Bukharin's *Theory of Historical Materialism*. This 'Popular Manual of Marxist Sociology', as it was sub-titled, was first published in 1921, and Gramsci probably used the French translation of 1927. He also knew of a famous paper 'Theory and Practice from the standpoint of dialectical materialism' which Bukharin read to the International Congress on the History of Science and Technology in London in 1931. It is ironical that, although in the early 1920s Bukharin certainly represented a major trend in Marxist orthodoxy, by the time Gramsci was writing about him he was already being criticized by Soviet writers, and within a few years was to be tried and executed on Stalin's instructions. In his belief in free discussion and in Marxism as a living and changing philosophy – 'It would be strange if Marxism ever stood still,' he wrote[2] – his views and those of Gramsci were very similar. And even in his practical policies he had, by the late 1920s, reached a view of the problem of the peasants not very dissimilar from that of Gramsci. But even if Gramsci's critique of Bukharin's *Historical Materialism* is sometimes unfair (and he probably had no direct knowledge of the contemporary discussions of Bukharin's views by, for example, György Lukàcs), his notes on Bukharin's work provide interesting evidence about the nature of Gramsci's theoretical Marxism and about his own intellectual preoccupations and assumptions.

There were three main criticisms which Gramsci made of Bukharin. First, he objected to Bukharin's distinction between history and sociology and his insistence that Marxism was a sociological rather than an historical theory. Second, he objected to Bukharin's insistence, similar to that of the nineteenth-century positivists, on natural science as the pattern to which all other forms of intellectual activity should conform. And, thirdly, he disliked Bukharin's attempt to reduce the dialectic to a mechanical principle of the equilibrium of forces. 'Sociology,' Gramsci wrote in a passage which combines all three of these criticisms,

> has been an attempt to create a method of historical and political science in a form dependent on a pre-elaborated philosophical system, that of evolutionist positivism . . . it became the philosophy of non-philosophers, an attempt to provide a schematic description and classification of historical and political facts, according to criteria built up on the model of natural science. It is therefore an attempt to define 'experimentally' the laws of evolution of human society in such a way as to 'predict' that the oak tree will develop out of the acorn. Vulgar evolution is at the root of sociology; and sociology cannot know the dialectical principle with its passage from quantity to quality . . . (QC p. 1432; PN p. 426)

It may be that this is an inaccurate description of what sociologists in fact set out to do – or at least sociologists since Comte and Herbert Spencer – but it reflects accurately enough Gramsci's view that history rather than sociology was the all-embracing subject that includes all others and precludes any mechanistic view of the development of human society. In this he followed Croce, deeply as he criticized him for not going far enough, for rejecting Marxism and for failing to see that if philosophy and history are identical, it must follow that politics and history and philosophy are identical also.

But Gramsci's objection to the reduction of history to sociology and the equation of Marxism with the sociological method is also linked to another of his fundamental attitudes, namely his 'voluntarism', his conviction that men could influence events, that historical developments

were not pre-ordained, that in history you could not necessarily predict that the oak tree would grow out of the
acorn. The reason for this particular objection to Bukharin's
views is an important one. Sociology, Gramsci thought,
was founded on empirically based statistical laws, and,
as such, could have some value. But, he went on,

> the fact has not been properly emphasized that statistical
> laws can be employed in the science and art of politics only
> so long as the great masses of the population remain . . .
> essentially passive in relation to the questions which interest
> historians and politicians. Furthermore the extension of
> statistics to the science and art of politics can have very
> serious consequences to the extent that it is adopted for
> working out future perspectives and programmes of action.
> In the natural sciences the worst that statistics can do is to
> produce blunders and irrelevancies which can easily be cor-
> rected by further research . . . But in the science and art of
> politics it can have literally catastrophic results which do
> irreparable harm. Indeed in politics the assumption of the
> law of statistics as an essential law operating of necessity
> is not only a scientific error, but becomes a practical error
> in action. (QC pp. 1429 – 30; PN pp. 428 – 9)

(One cannot help wondering whether he had some of
the disastrous results of Soviet planning in his mind.)

It was an essential element in Gramsci's political philosophy that the revolution, and indeed the preparation for
it, would involve a profound change in the consciousness
of the masses, because henceforth they would no longer
be the passive recipients of the measures of government
but a vital factor in the decisions about these measures,
in which they would themselves play a positive part. 'The
process,' as he put it, 'by which popular feeling is stan-
dardized ceases to be mechanical and casual (that is produced by the conditioning of environmental factors and
the like) and becomes conscious and critical.' (QC p. 1430;
PN p. 429) One of the problems for the reader of the

Notebooks is, of course, that, since his writing is fragmentary and disconnected, Gramsci was never obliged to deal with the contradictions in his work or to meet the objections that might be made to it, such as how his remarks about men ceasing to be statistical units and becoming participants in the decisions about their fate can be reconciled with the acceptance of the economic planning which is an essential element of Socialist society. However, certainly the notion of the Factory Councils and of participatory democracy in industry would have been for Gramsci part of the solution.

Bukharin's attempt to make Marxism the basis of a scientific sociology was criticized by Gramsci because of its neglect of an historical dimension and because of its attempt to apply the categories of natural science to human behaviour. But Gramsci also believed that Bukharin had misunderstood the nature and importance of the dialectical process. Bukharin was clearly rather embarrassed by the notion of the dialectic as adapted by Marx from Hegel. He felt that this was something which Marx had taken over too rapidly from the idealist school of philosophy, and if it were to find a place in a modern 'scientific' Marxism, it must be reduced to something more susceptible of scientific analysis. He therefore devoted little space to it, and, according to Gramsci, dealt with it 'in a very superficial manner'. Bukharin in fact was making a genuine attempt to reinterpret the theory of the dialectic in scientific terms, since even in the writings of Marx and Engels it had, as he wrote, 'the teleological flavour inevitably connected with the Hegelian formulation, which rests on the self-movement of spirit.' He believed that it could be reinterpreted in purely scientific language:

The world consists of forces, acting in many ways, opposing each other. These forces are balanced for a moment in exceptional cases only. We then have a state of 'rest' i.e.

their actual 'conflict' is concealed. But if we change only one of these forces, immediately the 'internal contradictions' will be revealed, equilibrium will be disturbed and if a new equilibrium is again established it will be on a new basis . . . It follows that the 'conflict', the 'contradiction' i.e. the antagonism of forces acting in various directions determines the motion of the system.[3]

For Gramsci, this kind of interpretation explained nothing, as it still made a distinction between that part of the world which could be explained in scientific terms and that part which was the subject of philosophy or metaphysics and so reduced philosophy 'to the level of a sub-species of formal logic and elementary scholastics'. (QC p. 1425; PN p. 435) But the whole point of Marxism for Gramsci was just that it had, for the first time in human experience, united the various aspects of life and thought – history, philosophy, politics, science – into a single system. 'The true fundamental function and significance of the dialectic,' he wrote,

can only be grasped if the philosophy of praxis is conceived as an integral and original philosophy which opens up a new phase of history and a new phase in the development of world thought. It does this to the extent that it goes beyond both traditional idealism and traditional materialism, philosophies which are expressions of past societies, while retaining their vital elements. If the philosophy of praxis is not considered except in subordination to another philosophy, then it is not possible to grasp the new dialectic through which the transcending of old philosophies is effected and expressed. (QC p. 1425; PN p. 435)

Gramsci's view of the dialectic has as much in common with Hegel as it does with Marx. Or, to put it another way, it is poised between Bukharin's view and that of Croce. He himself seems to have thought of the dialectic in three ways.[4] At its simplest it means the reciprocal interaction of one thing on another – the interaction, for example, of the intellectual or party leader and the masses whom he is both guiding and guided by – the perpetual dialogue that is inherent in every historical and political process. But, secondly, he also uses the term in a specifically Hegelian way, analysing historical developments in terms of the triad – thesis, antithesis, synthesis – and of the Hegelian 'negation of the negation'. 'In a sense, moreover,' he wrote in the Notebooks,

> the philosophy of praxis is a reform and a development of Hegelianism; it is a philosophy that has been liberated (or is attempting to liberate itself) from any unilateral or fanatical ideological elements; it is consciousness full of contradictions, in which the philosopher himself, understood both individually and as an entire social group, not only grasps the contradictions, but posits himself as an element of the contradiction and elevates this element to a principle of knowledge and therefore of action. (QC p. 1487; PN pp. 404 – 5)

This suggests the third meaning of the dialectic for Gramsci, which is of great importance for one of the central problems in his Marxism, the relation between the structure and superstructure. In the vulgar Marxism he was attacking and which he rather unfairly identified with Bukharin, the superstructure – ethics, law, philosophy, art, the whole realm of ideas – was directly conditioned by the economic system, by the means of production and exchange. Gramsci both instinctively and because of his own early philosophical training wanted to see historical change in more sophisticated terms and wanted to leave more room for the influence of ideas and indeed of individual men in the process of history. To do this he had to establish the basis for what Hegel had called the passage from quantity to quality, and to explain just how changes in material conditions could produce immaterial changes in men's consciousness, which in turn influenced future material developments. Bukharin, Gramsci maintained, by limiting the jump from quantity to quality to examples from the physical world contented himself

> with wordplay about water changing its state (ice, liquid, gas) with changes in temperature, a purely mechanical fact determined by external agents (fire, sun, evaporation of carbonic acid, etc.) . . . In the case of man, [he goes on] who is this external agent? . . . if every social aggregate is something more (and different) than the sum of its components, this must mean that the law or principle which explains the development of society cannot be a physical law, since in physics one does not get out of the quantitative sphere except metaphorically. (QC pp. 1446–7; PN p. 469)

Thus the dialectic is something more than the blind clash of physical forces. It is a movement to which man himself can contribute by becoming deliberately and of his own volition a force in the dialectical process. Once this is done, then the moment for the jump to a new kind of society and a new kind of consciousness has come. 'Every antithesis must necessarily place itself as a radical antagonist of the thesis, with the intention of destroying it completely and substituting for it completely'. (QC p. 1328) If Gramsci finds Bukharin's view of the dialectic too mechanical and positivistic, he has to take care to dissociate himself from the view held by Croce, in which the dialectic is merely action and reaction, challenge and response, so that the total negation of one historical stage by its successor is made into a painless process of reform, in which, as in liberal political theory, the role of ideology consists in laying down the forms and methods of the political struggle. For Gramsci, on the other hand, as for an earlier Hegelian revolutionary, Michael Bakunin, 'the urge to destroy is also a creative urge'. For him there was no easy road to revolution.

In his analysis of the transition from quantity to quality and of the relation between the structure and the superstructure, Gramsci relied heavily on certain texts of Marx and Engels themselves which he believed had been underestimated by some of their successors including Bukharin. The work of Marx which he quoted most frequently, and parts of which he clearly knew by heart, was the Introduction to the *Critique of Political Economy*. Marx had written in a famous passage:

> No social order ever perishes before all the productive forces for which there is room in it have developed; and new, higher relations of production never appear before the material conditions for their existence have matured in the womb of the old society.

It was a passage which to Gramsci seemed to illustrate the complexity of each historical situation, the unknown possibilities which it contained, since change was likely to be slow and the development of new forces not always predictable. Moreover, Marx had also written of revolutionary change:

> In considering such transformations a distinction should always be made between the material transformation of the economic conditions of production, which can be determined with the precision of natural science, and the legal, political, religious, aesthetic and philosophic – in short, ideological – forms in which men become conscious of this conflict and fight it out.

Engels, too, late in his life, in a text which Gramsci knew, had written of the way in which 'the reflections of . . . struggles in the minds of the participants . . . also exercise their influence upon the course of the historical struggles and in many cases preponderate in determining their form'.[5]

In asserting, therefore, 'the necessary reciprocity between structure and superstructure, a reciprocity which is nothing other than the real dialectical process', (QC pp. 1051 – 2; PN p. 366) Gramsci believed that he was in the true Marxist tradition. But perhaps he went further than any other Marxist thinker in recognizing the importance of the superstructure and the force of ideas in producing historical change, as well as seeing the impossibility of establishing any precise correlation between economic circumstances and intellectual developments :

The claim presented as an essential postulate of historical materialism, that every fluctuation of politics and ideology can be presented as an immediate expression of the structure must be contested in theory as primitive infantilism, and combated in practice with the authentic testimony of Marx, the author of concrete political and historical works. (QC p. 871; PN p. 407)

Lenin had believed that, within a historical pattern dictated by economic forces, there was room for many fluctuations :

World history reckons in decades. Ten or twenty years sooner or later makes no difference when measured by the scale of world history : from the standpoint of world history it is a trifle that cannot be calculated even approximately. But precisely for that reason it is a howling theoretical blunder to apply the scale of world history to practical politics.[6]

Gramsci developed this idea further in his Prison Notebooks; and no doubt his own political experiences over the past few years as well as his study of historical examples influenced his view. He made a distinction between 'organic' movements – the long-term trends in a society – and 'conjunctural' movements 'which appear as occasional, immediate, almost accidental'. (QC p. 1579; PN p. 177)

> When an historical period comes to be studied, the great importance of this distinction become clear. A crisis occurs, sometimes lasting for decades. This exceptional duration means that incurable structural contradictions have revealed themselves . . . and that, despite this, the political forces which are struggling to conserve and defend the existing structure . . . are making every effort to cure them within certain limits . . . These incessant and persistent efforts form the terrain of the 'conjunctural' . . . A common error in historical-political analysis consists in an inability to find the correct relationship between what is organic and what is conjunctural. This leads to presenting causes as immediately operative which in fact only operate indirectly, or to asserting that the immediate causes are the only effective ones. (QC pp. 1579 – 80; PN p. 178)

The attempt to analyse the relations between the structure and the superstructure and to describe the relationship between structural and conjunctural explanations led Gramsci to suggest an important, if obscure, idea, that of the 'historical bloc'. By this phrase he was trying to describe the moment when both objective and subjective forces combine to produce a situation of revolutionary change, the moment when the economic structure of the old order was collapsing but when there also were people with the will, determination and historical insight to take advantage of this. 'The conception of the historical bloc, in which precisely material forces are the content and ideologies are the form' is the way in which Gramsci described it. (QC p. 869; PN p. 377) And elsewhere he wrote that 'structures and superstructures form an "historical bloc"'. (QC p. 1051; PN p. 366) He believed that the realization that the objective material forces had reached a point where the revolution would be possible depended on a correct intellectual analysis, an all-embracing ideology which would give 'a rational reflection of the contradictions of the structure and [represent] the existence of the objective conditions for the revolutionizing of praxis'. (QC p. 1051; PN p. 366)

However, Gramsci also seems to have thought of the 'historical bloc' as something which was of psychological importance in the development of the character of the individual as well as sometimes of political importance in the development of societies. He used the term to describe the 'unity between nature and spirit (structure and superstructure) unity of opposites and of distincts'. (QC p. 1569; PN p. 137) And he also seems to have regarded the attainment of such unity within the psyche as a dialectical process similar to that which enabled men to influence the course of events in the external world. 'Men create their own personality,' he wrote,

1. by giving a specific personality and concrete ('national') direction to their own vital impetus or will.
2. by identifying the means which will make this will concrete and specific and not arbitrary.
3. by contributing to modify the ensemble of the concrete conditions for realizing this will to the extent of one's own limits and capacities and in the most fruitful form. Man is to be conceived as an historical bloc of purely individual and subjective or material elements with which the individual is in an active relationship. (QC p. 1338; PN p. 360)

9 Intellectuals; Machiavelli; 'Hegemony'

Gramsci's belief in the power of the will was not only reflected in the tenacity which he himself showed in continuing to think, to read and to write in spite of the hardships of prison life and the sufferings caused by his illnesses; it is also reflected in his comments on psycho-analysis and in the advice which he gave to his wife, who was living in Moscow and who suffered from recurrent psychological illness. He was interested in Freud and knew something of his theories, but he regarded their application as rather limited. 'To be sure, my knowledge of psycho-analysis is neither vast nor precise,' he wrote to his sister-in-law when discussing his wife's illness,

> but of the little I have studied I think there are at least a few points on which I can give a definite opinion . . . The most important point seems to be this: that a psycho-analytic cure can be helpful only to those elements in society which romantic literature used to call the 'insulted and injured' . . . those individuals who are caught up between the iron contrasts of modern life . . . people in short who fail to overcome warring contrasts of this nature and are incapable of arriving at a new moral serenity and tranquillity; i.e. an equilibrium between the impulse of the will and the ends which the individual can reach. The situation becomes dramatic at certain definite moments in history and in certain definite environments: when the environment is superheated to extreme tension, and gigantic collective forces are unleashed which press hard on single individuals . . . Such situations become disastrous for exceptionally refined and sensitive temperaments . . . I believe therefore that a person of culture, an active element in society (as Giulia certainly is . . .), is and must be his own best psycho-analyst.[1]

In a later letter, he elaborated and modified his views of the dialectic of the human psyche, pointing out that psychological crises not only affect 'the insulted and injured' but that they arise when the demands made by society conflict with 'an individual's actual tendencies, which are founded on the sedimentation of old habits and old ways of thinking'. If this tension cannot be resolved – for instance by a sceptical and hypocritical conformity with the demands of society –

the question can only be resolved in a catastrophic manner, because it gives rise to morbid outbreaks of repressed passion, which the necessary social 'hypocrisy' . . . has merely benumbed and driven deeper into its subconscious.[2]

This limited acceptance of such Freudian concepts as repression and the unconscious is combined in Gramsci with a Hegelian view of an ideal society in which the laws of the state and the dictates of the individual conscience or will coincide. But – and one cannot help feeling this is a direct product of his own prison experience – 'one can arrive at a certain serenity even in the clash of the most absurd contradictions and under the pressure of the most implacable necessity. But' – and here we come back to the central point of all Gramsci's philosophy –

one can only reach it if one succeeds in thinking 'historically', dialectically, and identifying one's own task with intellectual dispassionateness . . . In this sense . . . one can and therefore one must be 'one's own doctor'.[3]

Man can affect his own development and that of his own surroundings only in so far as he has a clear view of what the possibilities of action open to him are. To do this he has to understand the historical situation in which he finds himself : and once he does this, then he can play an active part in modifying that situation. The man of action is the true philosopher: and the philosopher must of necessity be a man of action:

> Man does not enter into relations with the natural world just by being himself part of it but actively by means of work and technique. Further: these relations are not mechanical. They are active and conscious . . . Each of us changes himself, modifies himself to the extent that he changes and modifies the complex relations of which he is the heart. In this sense, the real philosopher is, and cannot be other than the politician, the active man who modifies his environment, understanding by environment the ensemble of relations which each of us enters to take part in. If one's individuality is the ensemble of these relations, to create one's personality means to acquire consciousness of them, and to modify one's own personality means to modify the ensemble of these relations. (QC p. 1345; PN p. 352)

In both politics and individual behaviour, then, Gramsci believed that it was only through historical awareness and historical analysis, through an understanding of the precise historical circumstances in which societies and individual men found themselves that man's capacity to remake his surroundings and to remake himself become clear.

It is this attainment of historical awareness, the realization of what is the right course for himself and for the society in which he lives that makes the role of the intellectual all-important in Gramsci's theory of revolutionary change. However, Gramsci's discussion of the nature and role of intellectuals is by no means always easy to understand. This is partly because he uses the term in two ways. On the one hand, he writes of intellectuals in the usual sense as the intelligentsia who provide philosophy and ideology for the masses and who enable the ruling class to exercise their 'hegemony' by supplying the system of belief accepted by ordinary people so that they do not question the actions of their rulers. On the other hand,

Gramsci also writes that there is a sense in which everyone is an intellectual. By the exercise of a skill, by a knowledge of a language, every man demonstrates his capacity for intellectual activity:

> Each man . . . carries on some form of intellectual activity, that is, he is a 'philosopher', an artist, a man of taste, he participates in a particular conception of the world, has a conscious line of moral conduct and therefore contributes to sustain a conception of the world or to modify it, that is, to bring into being new modes of thought. (QC pp. 1550 – 1; PN p. 9)

But if everyone is an intellectual, how can one account for the existence of an intellectual class and define its role? Gramsci's answer seems to be to make a distinction between people who are intellectuals because this is an inevitable feature of their existence as human beings and those who perform the specific functions of intellectuals: 'All men are intellectuals . . . but not all men have in society the function of intellectuals. Thus, because it can happen that everyone at some time fries a couple of eggs or sews up a tear in his jacket, we do not necessarily say that everyone is a cook or a tailor.' (ibid.) In analysing those intellectuals who perform a specific social role, Gramsci makes another distinction which is also sometimes hard to follow – that between 'traditional' and 'organic' intellectuals. While the 'traditional' intellectuals are those we normally think of as such, the people who perform tasks of intellectual leadership in a given society, the 'organic' intellectuals are somehow more closely bound to the class to which they belong. As an example of the traditional intellectuals, Gramsci cites the clergy and their relation to the feudal governing class in the Middle Ages: they, it seems, were once an 'organic' intellectual class: 'The category of ecclesiastics can be considered the category of intellectuals organically bound to the landed aristocracy,' he writes. But as time goes on, intellectual groups which once performed an organic function, lose their links with a particular class and 'put themselves forward as autonomous and independent of the dominant social group'. (QC p. 1515; PN p. 7) In the case of the Catholic Church, this seems to have contributed to its survival in spite of changes in the ruling class in association with which it functions. The strength of the Church, Gramsci points out elsewhere, has lain in the fact that the higher intellectual stratum has not been separated from the lower. It is this which has allowed for modifications in doctrine to meet, by almost imperceptible stages, the demands of science or of new philosophical ideas. But, in times of social upheaval when the hold of the Church over the masses is weakened, then its role would seem, on Gramsci's account, to become ambiguous, with the clergy simply providing the opium of the masses in the interest of a social order with which the priests no longer have the organic ties which existed in the Middle Ages. As so often, this is one of the topics in the Prison Notebooks which Gramsci was unable to work out in detail, so that any attempt to summarize his ideas must be largely a surmise.

However, when writing of 'traditional' intellectuals other than the priesthood, Gramsci makes it quite clear that, as so often, it is Croce who is in his mind: 'The whole of idealist philosophy can easily be defined as the expression of that social Utopia by which the intellectuals think of themselves as "independent", autonomous, endowed with a character of their own.' (QC p. 1515; PN p. 8) But this feeling of independence is, of course, an illusion. Croce and other liberal idealist philosophers are inevitably linked to the class-structure of the society in which they live, and are as much bound to the industrialists – the ruling class of the liberal society of their day of whose liberalism they are the spokesmen – as the Catholic priesthood was to the feudal aristocracy.

The true duty of such traditional intellectuals should be, Gramsci implies, to behave as Marx and Engels had prescribed in the Communist Manifesto, that is to cut themselves adrift and join the revolutionary class, 'the class that has the future in its hands'. The organic intellectuals seem therefore to be those traditional intellectuals who have understood the direction in which history is moving and those intellectuals thrown up by the revolutionary class itself to serve as its leaders. As always, Gramsci, even at his most theoretical, is thinking in terms of his own experience or of the concrete historical examples with which he was familiar. The intellectual, organically linked to the revolutionary class, becomes a member of the political party which provides the leadership for that class. His role is essentially a practical one :

The mode of being of the new intellectuals can no longer consist in eloquence, which is an exterior and momentary mover of feelings and passions, but in active participation in practical life, as constructor, organizer, 'permanent persuader' and not just a simple orator. (QC p. 1551; PN p. 10)

However, the theoretical problem of linking the intellectual to the ordinary people, the Party to the masses, remained the same as it had been at the time of the Factory Council movement in Turin in 1919. As Gramsci wrote :

The position of the philosophy of praxis is the antithesis of that of catholicism. It does not tend to leave the 'simple' in their primitive philosophy of common sense, but rather to lead them to a higher conception of life. If it affirms the need for contact between intellectuals and 'simple' it is not in order to restrict scientific activity and preserve unity at the low level of the masses, but precisely in order to construct an intellectual-moral bloc which can make politically possible the intellectual progress of the mass and not only of small intellectual groups. (QC pp. 1384 – 5; PN pp. 332 – 3)

The role of the revolutionary party and the intellectuals who are its leaders was, in fact, to be much the same as that of the priesthood in the Catholic Church in its prime, when they were able to preserve 'the ideological unity of the entire social bloc which that ideology serves to cement and to unify'. (QC p. 1380; PN p. 328)

The influence of the intellectual, both as an active member of a political party in the contemporary revolutionary struggle and as a factor in past historical change, depended on his ability to remain in contact with the masses; otherwise he would become, to use a metaphor Gramsci often returned to, a member of a vanguard without an army to back it up, a general without followers. (In fact, he would be in the position to which Gramsci believed Bordiga had risked bringing the Italian Communist Party in 1923.) History was not made by 'intellectual élites separated from the masses', but rather by 'intellectuals who are conscious of being linked organically to a national-popular mass'. One has, Gramsci wrote,

to struggle against . . . the false heroisms and pseudo-aristocracies and stimulate the formation of homogeneous, compact social blocs, which will give birth to their own intellectuals, their own commandos, their own vanguard – who in turn will react upon those blocs in order to develop them. (QC p. 1676; PN pp. 204 – 5)

One of the great themes which Gramsci had proposed to treat, when he was optimistically outlining large intellectual projects at the outset of his time in prison, had been the role of the intellectuals in Italian history and Italian society. And although he was never able to write the extended systematic study of the subject which he had hoped to undertake, his reflections on Italian history

fill many pages in the Prison Notebooks. He was concerned naturally with the previous revolutionary period
in Italian history, that of the *Risorgimento*, of the creation
of Italian unity and the emergence of Italian liberalism, but
he was also fascinated by the political thought and the
historical development of the Italian Renaissance, and in
particular by the figure of Machiavelli.

Benedetto Croce had once called Marx 'the Machiavelli
of the proletariat',[4] and Gramsci, taking off from this suggestion, was determined to apply the kind of analysis
which Machiavelli had undertaken for sixteenth-century
Italy to contemporary society. Many pages of the Prison
Notebooks are devoted to 'Notes on Machiavelli', some
of them re-drafted in different versions; and one of the
many ambitious projects which Gramsci was prevented
by illness and imprisonment from carrying out was to
write a 'Modern Prince' which would provide for the
twentieth century the kind of political model or myth
which Machiavelli's *Prince* had suggested four hundred
years earlier. However, in the twentieth century, the role
of the Prince as the initiator and executant of political
change would be performed by the political party:

> The modern Prince, the Prince-myth, cannot be a real per-
> son, a concrete individual; it can only be an organism, a
> complex element of society, in which a collective will . . .
> begins to take concrete form. Such an organism has already
> been provided by historical development and it is the
> political party, the first cell in which germs of a collective
> will come together and tend to become universal and
> total. (QC p. 1558; PN p. 129)

Just as Machiavelli's aim was to educate the ruling class
of his day and force them to face the realities of the
political tasks facing Italy without being hampered by
the dogmas of the Church, so the 'Modern Prince' would
educate the proletariat and train it to become the ruling

class of the future. 'The greatness of Machiavelli,' Gramsci wrote, 'consists in having distinguished politics from ethics.' (QC pp. 749 – 50) Or rather, perhaps, to have divested politics of a false ethical content so that political leaders could move towards a society in which ethics and politics could once more coincide and in which there would be no conflict between them: 'Politics is conceived as a process which will open up into morality, that is it tends to open up into a form of association in which politics and morality will both have been transcended.' (QC p. 750) Here again, Gramsci comes close to Hegel's vision of a society in which there can be no conflict between public law and private conscience.

This is an idea which Gramsci was prepared to carry very far, and his interpretation of it shows how far he was from any libertarian or anarchistic view of society. He insists again and again that any political and economic reform must be accompanied by – and he uses the phrase dear to nineteenth-century social thinkers – an 'intellectual and moral reform'. The goal of such reform will be the voluntary acceptance by each individual of the values of the 'Modern Prince', of the Communist Party itself:

> The modern Prince, as it develops, revolutionizes the whole system of intellectual and moral relations, in that its development means precisely that any given act is seen as useful or harmful, as virtuous or as wicked, only in so far as it has as its point of reference the modern Prince itself, and helps to strengthen or to oppose it. In men's consciences, the Prince takes the place of the divinity or the categorical imperative, and becomes the basis for a modern laicism and for a complete laicization of all aspects of life and of all customary relationships. (QC p. 1561; PN p. 133)

The aim of the Party is to create a new political will. This, at least by the time he was writing the Prison Notebooks, Gramsci thought would take a long time. It was for this reason that, in the twentieth century, the revolution would be made by a collective body and not by an individual, whose action 'by its very nature cannot have a long-term and organic character'. (QC p. 1558; PN p. 129) As Gramsci reflected on the history of Italy and especially on the history of the previous century he was led to see the process of revolution as a much slower one than had seemed to be the case in the heady atmosphere of 1919 and 1920. As a result, he developed a theory that historical development, and especially revolutions, alternated between active and passive phases. Thus the upheavals of the French Revolution and the Napoleonic era had represented a time of active revolution which had been followed by a period of passivity. In 1848 there had again been a moment of active revolution, but later in the century, and especially after 1870, social changes had taken a different form. 'The same thing happens in the art of politics as in military art,' Gramsci wrote in one of those military metaphors of which he was fond. 'The war of movement becomes increasingly a war of position and one can say that a state wins a war according to how far it prepares it minutely and technically in the time of peace.' (QC pp. 1566 – 7; PN p. 243) In his period of active leadership of the Italian Communist Party, Gramsci had been concerned with giving the Party a mass base and with creating a situation in which the decisions of the Party leadership were accepted and understood by the rank and file members. Now, in his analysis of the role of the Party as the 'Modern Prince', and in his reflections on Machiavelli's historical role and on nineteenth-century Italian history, he was working out in a more theoretical way the strategy by which the revolution might be brought about. It was a strategy in which the war of position was as important as the war of movement. Indeed, it was essential for its success that the distinction between the two should be clearly observed. In making this point Gramsci criticizes the theory of 'permanent revolution', which he traces back to the revolution of 1848, but which had become particularly associated with Trotsky. He rejected the idea that there must never be a moment's respite in the progress of the revolution and that it would be fatal to pause before the revolution had been completely carried out.

> The formula [of 'permanent revolution'] is appropriate to a historical period in which the large mass political parties and the large economic unions did not exist and when society was so to speak still in a state of fluidity. (QC p. 1566; PN p. 243)

But later, as the power of the centralized state and of the mass organizations within it increases, the idea of permanent revolution is replaced by the idea of what Gramsci calls 'civil hegemony'. The establishment of such hegemony is essential for the success and survival of any ruling class. It is a central concept in Gramsci's political thinking, and the task of a revolutionary party, of the Modern Prince, is to establish such hegemony, if necessary by a slow modification of people's consciousness during a period of 'passive revolution' or a 'war of position'.

In developing his idea of 'hegemony' Gramsci explicitly acknowledged his debt to Lenin. Lenin, in his insistence that it was the duty of the Party to make clear to the masses the ideological bases of its policy, so that they would not be seduced by 'economism', by the prospect of immediate practical economic gain, had, Gramsci believed, made a philosophical contribution to the development of Marxism because he had stressed the importance of a change in consciousness in producing a revolution. Lenin had, Gramsci wrote,

> advanced philosophy as philosophy in so far as he had advanced political doctrine and practice. The realization of an apparatus of hegemony, in so far as it creates a new

ideological soil and determines a reform of consciousness and of the methods of knowledge, is a fact of knowledge, a philosophical fact. In Crocean language: when we succeed in introducing a new morality in conformity with a new conception of the world, we end up by introducing that conception of the world too, so that an entire reform of philosophy is brought about. (QC p. 1250; PN pp. 365 – 6)

It is arguable whether this is in fact what Lenin had been saying in texts like *What is to be done?* and *Two Tactics of Social Democracy in the Democratic Revolution*, but Gramsci had no doubt that the idea of achieving hegemony by means of a reform of consciousness was Lenin's major contribution to Marxist theory. It is also characteristic of his way of thinking that he tests his formulation of Lenin's view by immediately restating it in the language of Croce, so that his doctrine of hegemony seems to have the blessing of both his masters.

The hegemony of a political class meant for Gramsci that that class had succeeded in persuading the other classes of society to accept its own moral, political and cultural values. If the ruling class is successful, then this will involve the minimum use of force, as was the case with the successful liberal regimes of the nineteenth century.

The 'normal' exercise of hegemony in the area which has become classical, that of the parliamentary regime, is characterized by the combination of force and consensus which vary in their balance with each other, without force exceeding consensus too much. Thus it tries to achieve that force should appear to be supported by the agreement of the majority, expressed by the so-called organs of public opinion – newspapers and associations . . . Midway between consensus and force stands corruption or fraud (which is characteristic of certain situations in which the exercise of the function of hegemony is difficult, making the use of force too dangerous). (QC p. 1638)

In periods of crisis, such as that after the First World War, the apparatus of hegemony tends to break down : parties tended to fragment; no one group is able to obtain the consensus which would enable it to govern. The situation is ripe for a shift of power, for the creation of a new apparatus of hegemony and for the search for a new basis of consensus, or else, presumably, for a government by force.

A successful ruling class is one which before actually obtaining political power has already established its intellectual and moral leadership. To do this it must have as its core a homogeneous social group, but one which is also capable of attracting support from other groups. (Gramsci uses the example of the moderate liberals in the Italian *Risorgimento* who were able to attract support both from the intellectuals and from sections of the mass of the people, especially the peasants.) Moreover, the ruling group must to some extent respect the interests of others :

> The fact of hegemony undoubtedly presupposes that the interests and tendencies of the groups over which hegemony is to be exercised are taken into account, that there is a certain equilibrium of compromise, that, that is, the ruling group makes sacrifices of an economic-corporate kind, but it is also indubitable that such sacrifices and such compromises cannot affect what is essential. (QC p. 1591; PN p. 161)

There therfore seem to be two phases in the achievement of hegemony, each of which may take quite a long time. It is, as we have seen, a matter of long-term preparation in a 'war of position'. The period in which the cultural hegemony of a social group and its ideology is gradually established will be a period in which the party will act in co-operation with other groups and will, up to a point, respect their interests and make concessions to their demands. In this process, as in every historical change, the role of the intellectuals is for Gramsci all-important, since the achievement and maintenance of hegemony is largely a matter of education: 'Every relationship of "hegemony" is necessarily a pedagogic relationship.' (QC p. 1331; PN p. 350) The degree of success of such an educational process will be shown by the extent to which a new consensus or, to use Gramsci's phrase, a 'collective national will' is formed. In the past, it was the absence of such a will in Italy which caused Italy to be left out of some of the main developments in European history, such as the Reformation. To create such a will and form a 'popular national bloc' which will enable a new society to emerge, it is essential that the intellectual leaders do not lose touch with the masses, and that their ideas are subjected to the test of common sense. 'The error of the intellectual', Gramsci writes,

> consists in believing that it is possible to know without understanding and especially without feeling and passion . . . that the intellectual can be an intellectual . . . if he is distinct and detached from the people-nation [*popolo-nazione*], without feeling the elemental passions of the people, understanding them and thus explaining and justifying them in a particular historical situation, connecting them dialectically to the laws of history, to a superior conception of the world . . . History and politics cannot be made without passion, without this emotional bond between intellectuals and the people-nation. In the absence of such a bond the relations between intellectuals and the people-nation are reduced to contacts of a purely bureaucratic, formal kind; the intellectuals become a caste or a priesthood . . . (QC p. 1505; PN p. 418)

The role of the intellectual is therefore linked both to the nature of popular beliefs and popular sentiments and to the whole problem of internal democracy within the political party. Gramsci's old interest in popular culture was now combined with the preoccupations which he had felt at the time of the Factory Councils in Turin and with the need of uniting the leaders and the followers in what he called, in a term which for him clearly served many purposes, a 'historic bloc': 'If the relation between intellectuals and the people-nation,' the passage quoted above continues,

> between leaders and led, is the result of an organic participation in which feelings and passion become understanding and thence knowledge . . . then and only then is the relationship one of representation. Only then can there take place an exchange of individual elements between rulers and ruled, leaders and led, that is to say the realization of a life in common which alone is a social force, only then is the 'historic bloc' created. (QC p. 1505; PN p. 418)

Elsewhere Gramsci insists that there must be mobility between the ruling party and the masses: 'In the hegemonic system, there exists democracy between the leading group and the group which are led, to the extent to which the development of the economy and thus the legislation which expresses such development is favourable to the molecular passage from groups which are led to groups which lead.' (QC p. 1056) Gramsci was suspicious and impatient of bureaucracy, and he saw it as a great danger to any party that allowed itself to become too rigid, to become, as he put it, mummified and anachronistic. No doubt he remembered both the bureaucracy which had been characteristic of the Italian Socialist Party in his active days, but he also feared the danger, which Bordiga's view of the Communist Party had involved, that the leadership would be a self-appointed élite out of touch with the masses. Here again, the discussions in the Prison Notebooks provide general, rather abstract variations on themes with which Gramsci had been concerned during his active political career. When he looked at the bureaucracy of contemporary Italy, he saw that it was largely in the hands of the class whose volatility and opportunism made it always deeply suspect to him – the petty bourgeoisie, especially from the south of Italy, the very class to which his father had belonged. Such people were, Gramsci thought, determined to maintain their position and to prevent change at all costs. But for all his dislike and suspicion of bureaucracy and bureaucrats, he realized that both the state and the political party which performs functions within those areas of society which the state does not directly control, require some sort of administration. This must be flexible, democratic and disinterested. How these qualities were to be achieved was a problem of which Gramsci was very conscious without ever finding a precise answer. However, he suggests that the solution might lie – and here again he is saying much the same thing as he had been advocating in 1919 and 1920 – in a version of 'democratic centralism', which is, he wrote,

a 'centralism' in movement, to to speak, a continuous adaptation of the organization to the true movement, a blending of pressures from below with leadership from above, a continual insertion of elements which emerge from the depths of the masses into the solid framework of the directing apparatus which will ensure continuity and regular accumulation of experience. (QC p. 1634; PN p. 188 – 9)

This will provide, Gramsci thought, an 'organic' as opposed to that 'bureaucratic' centralism in which the ruling group tends to perpetuate itself and its privileges. It must be admitted that Gramsci's formulation remains highly metaphysical, indeed Hegelian, in language:

Democratic centralism offers an elastic formula which lends itself to many incarnations; . . . it consists in the critical search for what is similar in what is apparently different, and on the other hand for what is distinct or even opposite in what is apparently uniform, so as to co-ordinate and connect closely what is similar, but in such a way that the co-ordination and the connection appear to be a practical and 'inductive' necessity, experimental and not the result of a rationalistic deductive abstract process which is characteristic of pure intellectuals (or pure asses). (QC p. 1635; PN p. 189)

Like Sorel, whom he seems to be echoing here, Gramsci is never so much an intellectual as when he is attacking intellectuals, never so abstract as when he is praising the concrete. However, what he had in mind seems to have been something similar to what became the practice in Maoist China thirty years later, when intellectuals were obliged to do periods of manual labour: 'Unity of manual and intellectual work, and closer links between legislative and executive power (so that elected functionaries concern themselves not merely with the control of State affairs but also with their execution), may be motives of inspiration for a new approach in solving the problem of the intellectuals as well as the problem of functionaries.' (QC p. 1632; PN p. 186)

In the Prison Notebooks Gramsci was more concerned with analysing the past and with the search for historical laws than with prescribing specific courses of action for the future or planning the details of a new society which in the circumstances in which he was living must have seemed very remote. Nevertheless, as he realized that the revolution was still a long way off and that the capitalist order was still far from collapse, he became increasingly interested in the country in which capitalism seemed to be adapting itself most successfully to the demands of the twentieth century – the United States of America. One of his later notebooks was devoted to a collection of notes, many of them copies or new drafts of earlier ones, which he himself headed 'Americanism and Fordism'.

Gramsci believed that the industrialists in America had certain advantages over those in Europe, because they were able to operate within a simpler social structure which had, he thought, something in common with the Europe of an earlier age, while at the same time having the advantages of modern organization and modern technology. America, he shrewdly observed, had much in common with the society predicted in the early nineteenth century by Henri de Saint-Simon, so that he saw, for example, Rotarianism as a kind of modern Saint-Simonianism of the Right, which advocated the view that 'industry and trade, before being business, are a social *service*'. (QC p. 541)

The main advantage which the United States had over Europe, and especially over Italy, was that there were far fewer people who were not directly engaged in the process of production. In America, Gramsci writes, there do not exist numerous classes without an essential function in the world of production, that is totally parasitic classes. European 'tradition', European 'civilization' is on the other hand characterized by the existence of such classes, created by the 'richness' and 'complexity' of past history which has left a pile of passive sediment through the phenomena of saturation and fossilization of the state officials and of the intellectuals, of the clergy and the landed proprietors, of predatory commerce and of the army . . . We can say therefore that the older the history of a country, the more numerous and burdensome is this sedimentation of a mass of useless idlers who live on the 'inheritance' of their 'ancestors', of these pensioners of economic history. (QC p. 2141; PN p. 281)

America, on the other hand, does not have to support such a burden. The industrialists can keep up their rate of profit, because, Gramsci believed, they do not have to support innumerable middlemen and parasites – though he sees signs that the wives and daughters of American businessmen are becoming just such a useless class. The industrialists are the ruling class in a very direct sense : 'hegemony is born in the factory and to be exercised requires a minimal number of political and ideological intermediaries'. (QC p. 2146; PN p. 285)

At the same time, the ideas and practice of Henry Ford and the teachings of the engineer Frederick W. Taylor, who pioneered new methods for the organization of labour in the factories, enabled a high rate of productivity to be maintained. This was achieved, not only by the payment of high wages to skilled workers but also by attempts to control all aspects of the workers' lives. Prohibition, Gramsci believed, had been introduced simply because it was in the interests of the industrialists to reduce the number of hours of work lost through drunkenness. In Ford's factories the sexual behaviour of the workers was scrutinized to make sure that it did not impair their efficiency. Although the process had not yet gone very far there were nevertheless signs that rationalization in the use of labour and of the means of production had led to 'the necessity of developing a new human type, in conformity with the new type of labour and of the productive process'. (QC p. 2146; PN p. 286) The evolution of a new type of capitalist man might, on this view, delay the development of socialist man.

It is interesting that Gramsci thought that the insistence on rationalization and efficient management in industry which he regarded as characteristic of American capitalism was similar to the kind of planning and organization of heavy industry which Trotsky had advocated in the Soviet Union in the early 1920s. The essence of Trotsky's proposals, Gramsci wrote,

> consisted in an 'over'-resolute (and therefore not rationalized) will to give supremacy in national life to industry and to industrial methods, to accelerate, through coercion imposed from outside, the growth of discipline and order in production, and to adapt habits to the necessity of work. Given the general way in which all the problems connected with this tendency were conceived, it was destined necessarily to end up in a form of Bonapartism. Hence the inexorable necessity of crushing it . . . The principle of coercion, direct or indirect, in the ordering of production and work is correct . . . but the form which it assumed was mistaken. (QC p. 2146; PN p. 301)

Gramsci does not elaborate on whether the American system will end up as some sort of 'Bonapartist' dictatorship, or how such a development is to be avoided in a socialist state, but he implies that the difference between socialist regulation of labour and the capitalist methods of control practised in America lies in the ideology which inspires it. 'The new methods of production are indissoluble from a certain way of life, of thought, of experiencing life : it is not possible to obtain successes in one field without obtaining tangible results in the other.'

(QC p. 2164; PN p. 301)

Throughout the Prison Notebooks, whether Gramsci is analysing Italian history, criticizing Croce, discussing the function of the political party or the nature of the ruling class, he was always stressing that any major historical change, any emergence of a new élite, was marked by an intellectual and moral reform, by a change in men's consciousness. At the same time he was obsessed by the dilemmas which had confronted him in his practical political life, by the dialectical clash between freedom and discipline, between personal liberty and economic and administrative efficiency. And although his discussion of the present and the future is nearly always vague and generalized, especially since he was precluded by the fact of his imprisonment from criticizing the Fascist regime or from giving a blue-print for a future revolution, we can perhaps begin to see how the Prison Notebooks have suggested methods of political action and forms of political analysis which have made his influence on political life in Italy so strong many years after his death.

Although Gramsci showed much knowledge of French history and politics and considerable insight into English and American culture, it was with Italy that he was primarily concerned and it was from the Italian past that he drew the detailed examples which illustrate his historical analysis, details of a kind which are necessarily absent from his discussion of the present. However, his historical studies and his own direct experience of the Comintern meant that he was always aware of international influences and international comparisons. He believed, for example, that hegemony could be exercised on an international scale, as well as within a single country. It is, he wrote, a relationship which 'occurs not only within a nation, between the various forces of which the nation is composed, but in the international and world-wide fields, between complexes of international and continental civilizations'. (QC p. 1331; PN p. 350) Such a view allows historically for, for example, the foreign ascendancy over Italian culture in the sixteenth century, and, although Gramsci did not say so explicitly, for the leadership of the Soviet Union in the Communist International as he had experienced it. Indeed, Gramsci asked a series of questions on this topic, which, as with so many others, he left unanswered:

> Is the cultural hegemony by one nation over another still possible? Or is the world already so united in its economic and social structure that a country, if it can have 'chronologically' the initiative in an innovation cannot keep its 'political' monopoly and so use such a monopoly as the basis of hegemony? What significance therefore can nationalism have today? Is it not possible as economic and financial 'imperialism' but not as civil 'primacy' and political and intellectual hegemony? (QC p. 1618)

One wonders how he would have viewed the respective positions of the United States and the Soviet Union in the second half of the twentieth century, or what he would have said about the possession of nuclear weapons.

It is, however, because of Gramsci's insistence on the special features of Italian history as well as his personal links through Palmiro Togliatti with the Italian Communist Party as it has developed since the Second World War that the Italian Communists have been preoccupied with the interpretation of Gramsci's writings as a guide to their own theory and tactics, and it is indeed striking how much of his analysis of the situation fifty years ago still seems relevant:

> The crisis presents itself practically in the growing difficulty of forming governments and in the ever-growing instability of the governments themselves: this has its immediate origins in the multiplication of parliamentary parties and in the permanent internal crises of each of these parties . . . The forms of this phenomenon are also to some extent

those of corruption and moral dissolution: each fraction of the party thinks it has the infallible recipe to stop the enfeeblement of the entire party and has recourse to every means to win leadership or at least to share in leadership of it, just as in parliament the party believes it is the only one which should form a government to save the country, or at least claims, if it gives its support to the government, the right to participate in it as widely as possible; hence detailed quibbling negotiations which are necessarily involved with personalities to an extent that they seem scandalous, and which are often treacherous and in bad faith. Perhaps in reality the personal corruption is less than it seems, since the whole political organism has been corrupted by the decay of the function of hegemony. (QC p. 1639)

Gramsci wrote this as an account of French political life in the 1920s; but it is an extraordinarily accurate description of the state of the Italian Christian Democrat Party in the 1970s.

Equally, the Italian Communists can perhaps claim that they are well on the way to establishing their hegemony with the collapse of the old hegemonic system. They have achieved a dominant position in local government in many areas and in so far as they attract support not only from organized labour but also from very many intellectuals and professional people, they seem to be establishing their hegemony very much along the lines which Gramsci had suggested. However, in spite of the use that has sometimes been made of his writings by contemporary Communists, it would be a mistake to think of Gramsci as providing a guide to revolutionary methods or a key to a successful revolution any more than Marx did. Like Marx himself, Gramsci in the Prison Notebooks was more concerned to reach a general understanding of the nature of historical, social and economic change and of the role of the intellectual and the political party in it. Moreover, like many revolutionary thinkers, and again like Marx himself, he was more interested in the long-term process by which the revolution would come about than in what society would look like after the revolution. Gramsci wanted to write neither a handbook for revolutionaries nor a description of a future Utopia.

Gramsci was deeply interested in the relation of Marxism to the old intellectual and social order; and indeed, partly no doubt because of his respect for the Catholic Church, he knew how tenacious old ideologies could be. He had always been fascinated by the relationship of Croce to Marx and the way in which Croce had been able to use Marx for his own purposes. 'One can say,' Gramsci wrote, 'that a great part of the philosophical work of B. Croce represents an attempt to absorb the philosophy of praxis and to incorporate it into an ancillary of traditional culture.' (QC p. 1435) This is, he thought, both a sign that Marxism was beginning to exercise its own hegemony within the system of traditional culture, and a demonstration of the strength of the old order. While Marxism, Gramsci believed (though his own use of Croce hardly bears this out), does not need any outside support, the old culture 'which is still robust and above all is more refined and polished tries to react like conquered Greece and end up by conquering the coarse Roman conqueror'. (QC p. 1435)

It is because of this awareness of the interaction of Marxism with other philosophies and of the importance of gradual cultural transformations that Gramsci's writing has such an attraction for non-Marxists. Although, like all true believers, Gramsci would have repudiated the suggestion that Marxism was just one ideology among many from which people could choose those elements which suit them, it is nevertheless tempting to consider Gramsci's own notebooks in such terms. Because of their variety as well as their fragmentary nature they provide texts to support many different views of Gramsci's message as well as raising innumerable questions to which, on account of the circumstances of his life, Gramsci could not give an answer. His range of interests, the extraordinary breadth of his own reading and of his historical and philosophical culture as well as the enforced detachment with which he was writing his more theoretical work make him unique among Marxists. At the same time the fact that he remained rooted in the Italian and the European idealist cultural tradition so that, however much he reacted against them, Vico and Hegel, Sorel and Croce were in some ways as important for him as Marx and Lenin, means that it is easier for the non-Marxist to conduct a dialogue with Gramsci than with any other Marxist writer of the twentieth century.

During his lifetime Gramsci was largely isolated from those contemporary Marxists outside Italy with whom he might have had most in common and, since his most important theoretical work remained unpublished till some years after his death, they had little opportunity for studying his ideas. Nor does he seem to have been much influenced by them. Few are mentioned in the Prison Notebooks beyond Lenin, Trotsky, Bukharin and an occasional reference to Stalin. Gramsci admired Rosa Luxemburg, who was murdered in 1919, as a martyr for the revolutionary cause comparable to the martyrs in the history of Christianity, but it was as a theorist of revolutionary methods rather than the severe exponent of Marxian economics that he respected her. He knew and was impressed by Rosa Luxemburg's pamphlet on the Mass Strike, written in 1906 but only translated into Italian in 1919, and he had read an early article of hers on Stagnation and Progress in Marxism which was reprinted in a French translation in 1928, in which she put forward the idea that each aspect of Marxist philosophy is developed in a different way at different times according to the tactical needs of practical political activity. Gramsci carried this argument further to suit his own conception of historical change, and he believed that a further development in

Marxism would be necessary that would simultaneously raise the level of popular culture and popular understanding of Marxist teaching while at the same time being of sufficient subtlety and sophistication to convince the liberal intellectuals of the correctness of the Marxist analysis. Gramsci certainly shared Luxemburg's insistence on the necessity of spontaneous mass support for the revolution, and he believed that the Turin Factory Councils in 1919 were putting into practice some of her ideas about how to make the revolution.

The Marxist theorists of his own generation who shared some of Gramsci's preoccupations were the Hungarian György Lukàcs and the German Karl Korsch. Gramsci himself admitted that he knew Lukàcs's work only vaguely, though it is likely that he had read his essay on Rosa Luxemburg as a Marxist and one or two other works. Both men were more aware than most Marxists of the importance of cultural and philosophical factors in interpreting the doctrine of historical materialism. Both of them recognized and stressed the element of Hegelian idealism in Marx. However, Gramsci was not preoccupied, as Lukàcs was, with developing a Marxist aesthetic and literary theory, and he was freed by the circumstances of his life and death from the necessity of surviving in Moscow throughout the Stalinist period, so that he was certainly a more consistent as well as a wider-ranging thinker than Lukàcs ever was.

In Germany in the early 1920s Karl Korsch, a university lecturer in jurisprudence and briefly active in Communist politics before breaking with the Party, was formulating in a theoretical way some of the ideas which Gramsci had tried to put into practice in the Factory Council movement, and stressing that socialization should not mean centralization and that the Factory Councils must be the necessary base for any true revolution. But Korsch, although his writings have been re-discovered in the years since 1961 when he died, a sad and disappointed exile in

the United States, was never more than the spokesman
for a tiny sect, so that his work, for all its interest, has not
had the resonance which Gramsci's has achieved. There
was never any contact between the two men; and in fact,
by the mid-1920s, Korsch, because of his quarrel with the
Communist International, had more sympathy with Bordiga's position than with that of Gramsci since both
Korsch and Bordiga seemed to be representative of a
small minority resisting the attempts of Stalin and the
Communist Party of the Soviet Union to dominate the
International Communist Movement.

For all his genuine internationalism and the wide range
of his reading Gramsci remained a deeply Italian figure,
continuing the particular Italian brand of Marxism which
Antonio Labriola had begun in the nineteenth century.
Gramsci was in some ways a lonely thinker, isolated first
by the pressure of day-to-day journalism and political
work, and then by his imprisonment. It is this which gives
the Prison Notebooks their freshness. One has the feeling
that Gramsci arrives at his conclusions entirely on his
own from direct reflection on the multifarious texts he
was reading and on his own political and personal experiences. Even when his ideas are similar to those of
other thinkers, he comes to them in his own way after
criticizing and reacting to the works he has been studying. In contrast to the sharp polemical and public tone
of his earlier journalism the Prison Notebooks have the
detached and contemplative quality of work written for
the author alone in order to clarify his thought and to
be the basis of the great systematic works he never lived
to write.

Although Gramsci often suggests ways in which a
dialogue can be conducted between Marxism and other
philosophies, and although there are aspects of his thought
which are closer to the critical philosophy of Hork-
heimer, Adorno and the Frankfurt School than they are
to the dogmatic systems of Lenin or Rosa Luxemburg

or György Lukàcs, it would be wrong to think of Gramsci as primarily concerned with the problems of sociology and epistemology in the convoluted abstract fashion of the Frankfurt School, in whose writings there is so rarely a concrete historical example. Gramsci's abstract thought was largely the product of his imprisonment and of his enforced withdrawal from active politics. His ideology remained one of action; it was always a 'philosophy of praxis'. Moreover, the basic structure of his thought and the core of his emotional and political commitment were undoubtedly Marxist, and it would be wrong to suggest that he ever envisages a non-Marxist road to Socialism or that he ever really thinks that any philosophical system other than Marxism can be an adequate basis either for explaining or changing the world. The ways by which Gramsci hoped that people would come to accept the 'philosophy of praxis' as the basis for their lives and the hegemony of the Communist Party as the basis for the state are more humane than those employed by Lenin or Stalin, but one must not think that Gramsci was ever just a democratic reformist Socialist prepared to work indefinitely within the existing political and constitutional framework. His followers talk of the need for a 'historic compromise' with other social and political forces, but it is hard to think of this compromise as being other than tactical. 'The most important observation to be made about any concrete analysis of the relations of force is the following', so a key passage in Gramsci's notes on Machiavelli runs,

That such analyses cannot and must not be ends in themselves (unless the intention is merely to write a chapter of past history), but acquire significance only if they serve to justify a particular practical activity or initiative of will. They reveal the points of least resistance, at which the force of will can be most fruitfully applied; they suggest immediate tactical operations; they indicate how a campaign of agitation may best be launched, what language will best be understood by the masses, etc. The decisive element in every situation is the permanently organized and long-prepared force which can be put in the field when it is judged that a situation is favourable . . . Therefore the essential task is that of systematically and patiently ensuring that this force is formed, developed and rendered ever more homogeneous, compact and self-aware. This is clear from military history and from the care with which in every period armies have been prepared in advance to be able to make war at any moment. The Great Powers have been great precisely because they were at all times prepared to intervene effectively in favourable international conjunctures – which were precisely favourable because there was the concrete possibility of effectively intervening in them. (QC pp. 1588 – 9; PN p. 185)

If this force exists in the form of the Italian Communist Party today, then Gramsci also saw how the conduct of a successful campaign lies in making appropriate alliances at the right time :

An appropriate political initiative is always necessary to liberate the economic thrust from the fetters of traditional politics, the change of political direction of certain forces which must be absorbed if a new homogeneous politico-economic historic bloc without internal contradictions is to be achieved . . . If the union of two forces is necessary to defeat a third, a recourse to arms and coercion (even supposing that these are available) is nothing but a methodical hypothesis and the only concrete possibility is a compromise since force can be used against enemies but not against a part of one's own side which we want to assimilate rapidly and whose 'good will' and enthusiasm are needed. (QC pp. 1612 – 13; PN p. 168)

The Communist Party, Gramsci always believed, needs as broad a base as possible. It can, as he envisaged in 1923, include an alliance with the peasants : it can hope to win over some of the intellectuals and some of the petty bourgeoisie, but it remains a Communist Party all the same. Yet Gramsci was too good a student of Vico not to appreciate the ironies of history, and he understood the way in which men's ideas and goals are modified by their own wills, by their own experiences, by changes in the economic substructure which they could not possibly have foreseen. 'We know what has happened and not what will happen, which is "non-existent" and therefore unknowable by definition.' (QC p. 1404; PN p. 438) He would have certainly been prepared to see an Italian Communist Party following a specifically Italian line and not slavishly imitating the tactics and methods adopted elsewhere. He would have been impressed by the capacity for survival which the capitalist system has shown in the years since his death.

But Gramsci never claimed to be a prophet and it is fruitless to treat his texts as if they were the sayings of an oracle which will predict the future for us. We will read his Prison Notebooks, the incomparable letters from prison, even his journalism, to increase our understanding of the past and thus to give us greater insight into the present. But we will read Gramsci even more because his writings are the work of an exceptionally intelligent man of our own time whose life and thought show how it is possible for the human will to transcend the limitations both of historical and of personal circumstance. The greatest Marxist writer of the twentieth century, paradoxically, is also one of the greatest examples of the independence of the human spirit from its material limitations.

Notes

INTRODUCTION

1. Louise Althusser, *For Marx* (London, 1969) p. 114.
2. Antonio Gramsci, *Letters from Prison* (New York, 1973) p. 193; *Lettere del Carcere* (Turin, 1965) p. 390.
3. E. J. Hobsbawm, 'The Great Gramsci', *New York Review of Books*, Vol. XXI, No. 5, 4 April 1974.

PART I

1. ORIGINS

1. There is an excellent account of Gramsci's family background and early life in Giuseppe Fiori, *Vita di Antonio Gramsci*, (Bari, 1965), translated by Tom Nairn as *Antonio Gramsci, Life of a Revolutionary* (London, 1970).
2. Fiori, op. cit., English edition, p. 39.
3. Antonio Gramsci, *La Questione Meridionale*, ed. Franco de Felice and Valentino Parlato (Rome, 1970) p. 140.
4. Fiori, op. cit., p. 70.
5. 'Preludio', *Avanti!* 17 May 1916: *Scritti Giovanili (1914-18)* (Turin, 1958) p. 37.
6. 'Marinetti rivoluzionario?', *L'Ordine Nuovo* 5 January 1921: *Socialismo e Fascismo: L'Ordine Nuovo (1921-22)* (Turin, 1967) p. 22.
7. 'Piazza della Pace', *Avanti!* 8 May 1961: *Scritti Giovanili (1914-18)* p. 35.
8. All quotations from the 1975 edition of the *Quaderni del Carcere* are referred to as QC in the text. Where these passages are included in the English *Selections from the Prison Notebooks* I have also given the reference to this volume as PN, although I have occasionally preferred my own translation.
9. Fiori, op. cit., p. 74; *Lettere del Carcere* p. 466. See Carlo Cicerchia, 'Il rapporto col Leninismo e il problema della rivoluzione italiana', and Emile Agazzi, 'Filosofia della prassi e filosofia dello spirito', both in Alberto Caracciolo and Gianni Scalia (eds.), *La Città Futura: Saggi sulla figura e il pensiero di Antonio Gramsci* (Milan, 1959).
10. *Quaderni della Critica* 10, 1948, pp. 78-9. See Eugenio Garin,

'Antonio Gramsci nella cultura italiana', *Studi Gramsciani*: Atti del convengo tenuto a Roma nei giorni 11-13 gennaio 1958 (Rome, 1959) p. 3.

11. Unsigned article, 11 October 1919: *L'Ordine Nuovo (1919-20)* (Turin, 1954) pp. 460-1.
12. Quoted in Leonardo Paggi, *Gramsci e il Moderno Principe: I. Nella crisi del socialismo italiano* (Rome, 1970) p. 127.
13. Fiori, op. cit., p. 92.
14. Fiori, op. cit., p. 88.

2. THE SOCIALIST PARTY

1. *La Città Futura* 11 February 1917: *Scritti Giovanili (1914-18)* p. 78.
2. Antonio Gramsci, *Letteratura e Vita Nazionale* (Turin, 1950) p. 307, quoted in L. Paggi op. cit., p. 179. See also Guido Davico Bonino, *Gramsci e il Teatro* (Turin, 1972).
3. *Lettere del Carcere* p. 370.
4. Antonio Gramsci, *Sotto la Mole* (1916-20) (Turin, 1960) pp. 268-9.
5. 'Socialismo e cultura', *Il Grido del Popolo* 29 January 1916: *Scritti Giovanili* pp. 25-6.
6. Unsigned article, December 1920: *L'Ordine Nuovo 1919-20* p. 493. See also L. Paggi, op. cit., pp. 218ff.
7. *Lettere del Carcere* pp. 791, 808.
8. 'Libero pensiero e pensiero libero', *Il Grido del Popolo* 15 June 1918: *Scritti Giovanili* p. 261.
9. 'Dopo il congresso socialista spagnuolo', 13 November 1915: *Scritti Giovanili* p. 7. See also Ezio Avigdor, 'Il movimento operaio torinese durante la prima guerra mondiale' in Caracciolo and Scalia, op. cit.
10. 'I Massimalisti russi', *Il Grido del Popolo* 28 July 1918: *Scritti Giovanili* p. 124.
11. Palmiro Togliatti, 'Il Leninismo nel pensiero e nell'azione di Antonio Gramsci', *Studi Gramsciani*: Atti del convengo tenuto a Roma nei giorni 11-13 gennaio 1958 (Rome, 1959).
12. 'La Rivoluzione contro il "Capitale"', *Avanti!* 24 November 1917: *Scritti Giovanili* pp. 149-153.

3. THE FACTORY COUNCIL MOVEMENT

1. See Introduction to *Socialismo e Fascismo: L'Ordine Nuovo 1921-22*.
2. 'Democrazia operaia', 21 June 1919: *L'Ordine Nuovo* p. 10. On the Council movement, see especially Gwyn A. Williams,

Proletarian Order: Antonio Gramsci, Factory Councils and the Origins of Communism in Italy 1911-21 (London, 1975). For the whole of this period of Gramsci's career, the pioneering study by John M. Cammett, *Antonio Gramsci and the Origins of Italian Communism* (Stanford, 1967) is most valuable.

3. 'Sindicati e consigli', 11 October 1919: *L'Ordine Nuovo* p. 36.
4. 'Per un rinnovamento del partito socialista', 8 May 1920: *L'Ordine Nuovo* pp. 121-2.
5. 'Democrazia operaia', 21 June 1919: *L'Ordine Nuovo* p. 12.
6. The detailed organization was printed in *L'Ordine Nuovo* on 8 November 1919. See the discussion in Gwyn A. Williams, op. cit., Ch. 5.
7. Unsigned article in *L'Ordine Nuovo* 23 August 1919. See Alberto Caracciolo, 'Serrati, Bordiga e la polemica Gramsciana contro il "blanquismo" o settarismo di partito' in Caraccolio and Scalia, op. cit., p. 230.
8. Paolo Spriano, *Storia del Partito Comunista Italiano*, I. *Da Bordiga a Gramsci* (Turin, 1967) p. 12.
9. Controllo di classe', 3 January 1920: *L'Ordine Nuovo* p. 249. See Franco de Felice, *Serrati, Bordiga, Gramsci e il Problema della Rivoluzione in Italia 1919-20* (Bari, 1971) p. 356.
10. 'Per un rinnovamento del partito socialista', 8 May 1920: *L'Ordine Nuovo* p. 117.
11. Quoted in Spriano, op. cit., I p. 53. See also Tomaso Detti, *Serrati e la Formazione del Partito Cumunista Italiano* (Rome, 1972) p. 35.
12. *Avanti!* 2 September 1920, quoted in L. Paggi, op. cit., p. 321. 321.

4. THE COMMUNIST PARTY

1. Camilla Revera, quoted in Spriano, op. cit., p. 249 fn. 1.
2. G. M. Serrati, 'Riposta di un comunista unitario al compagno Lenin' quoted in Cammett, op. cit., p. 135.
3. 'Il sviluppo della rivoluzione', 13 September 1919: *L'Ordine Nuovo* pp. 30-32. See Gwynn A. Williams, *Proletarian Order*, pp. 114ff. for a detailed discussion of this document.
4. 'Pulcinella', 16 April 1921: *L'Ordine Nuovo* p. 354.
5. *L'Ordine Nuovo* 28 March 1922: *Socialismo e Fascismo* p. 521.
6. 'Il compagno G. M. Serrati e le generazioni del socialismo italiano', *L'Unità* 14 May 1926, in Giansiro Ferrata and Niccolo Gallo (eds.) *2000 Pagine di Gramsci I. Nel tempo della lotta (1914-26)* (Milan, 1964) p. 770.
7. 'Bergsoniano!', *L'Ordine Nuovo* 2 January 1921: *Socialismo e*

Fascismo p. 13.

8. 'Capacita politica', *Avanti!* 24 September 1920: *L'Ordine Nuovo* p. 171. English translation in *The New Edinburgh Review*, 3 special issues on Gramsci 1974, II, pp. 110-11.
9. 'Discorso agli anarchici': *L'Ordine Nuovo* p. 396.
10. ibid. pp. 400-401.
11. Sindicalismo e consigli', 8 November 1919: *L'Ordine Nuovo* p.48.

5. FASCISM

1. 'Forze elementari', *L'Ordine Nuovo* 26 April 1921: *Socialismo e Fascismo* p. 151.
2. *L'Ordine Nuovo* 11 May 1921, quoted in Spriano, op. cit., I p. 166 n. 5.
3. 'Dialettica reale', *L'Ordine Nuovo* 3 March 1921: *Socialismo e Fascismo* p. 860.
4. 'Cos'è la reazione', *Avanti!* 24 November 1920: *L'Ordine Nuovo* p. 366.
5. 'Italia e Spagna', *L'Ordine Nuovo* 11 March 1921: *Socialismo e Fascismo* p. 101.
6. 'La crisi italiana', (Report to Central Committee of Italian Communist Party 13-14 August 1924) in *La Costruzione del Partito Comunista* (Turin, 1971) p. 33.
7. 'Politica fascista', *L'Ordine Nuovo* 25 May 1921: *Socialismo e Fascismo* pp. 167-8.
8. 'Legalità', *L'Ordine Nuovo* 28 August 1920: *Socialismo e Fascismo* p. 306. See also Paggi, op. cit., p. 372.
9. See Thomas A. Bates, 'Gramsci and the Theory of Hegemony', *Journal of the History of Ideas*, vol. XXXVI, No. 2, April-June 1975.
10. 'La crisi italiana', *L'Ordine Nuovo* 1 September 1924: *La Costruzione del Partito Comunista* pp. 30-31.
11. To Zino Zini, quoted in Spriano, op. cit., p. 343.
12. To Giulia, 6 March 1924, *2000 Pagine di Gramsci*: II pp. 23-4.
13. To Zino Zini, quoted in Spriano, op. cit., p. 343.
14. Quoted in Spriano, op. cit., I p. 305.
15. Quoted in Spriano, op. cit., I p. 483.
16. Quoted in Spriano, op. cit., I p. 279.
17. Gramsci's speech was printed in *L'Unità* 23 May 1925. Reprinted in *La Costruzione del Partito Comunista* p. 85.
18. Quoted in Spriano, op. cit., I p. 441.
19. *2000 Pagine di Gramsci* I p. 832.
20. Paolo Spriano, op. cit., II: *Gli anni della clandestinà* (Turin, 1969) p. 55.

6. THE LYONS THESES AND THE SOUTHERN QUESTION

1. Piero Gobetti, *Scritti Politici* (Turin, 1960) p. 1003.
2. 'Clerici ed agrari', *Avanti!* 7 July 1916, in Antonio Gramsci, *La Questione Meridionale*, op. cit.
3. 'Operai e contadini', *L'Ordine Nuovo* 3 January 1920: op. cit., p. 72.
4. Report to Central Committee of Italian Communist Party, quoted in Spriano, op. cit., I p. 470.

PART II

7. PRISON

1. To his mother, 23 September 1929, *Letters from Prison* p. 153.
2. To Tatiana, 7 September 1931, *Letters from Prison*, p, 203; *Lettere del Carcere* p. 480.
3. To Tatiana, 19 March 1927, *Letters from Prison* pp. 89-90; *Lettere del Carcere* p. 58.

8. HISTORICAL MATERIALISM AND THE DIALECTIC

1. 'Il programma de L'Ordine Nuovo', *L'Ordine Nuovo* April 1924: *La Costruzione del Partito Comunista* (Turin, 1971) p. 21.
2. Quoted in Stephen F. Cohen, *Bukharin and the Bolshevik Revolution* (London, 1974) p. 107. This excellent biography gives a more sympathetic interpretation of Bukharin's views than that of Gramsci.
3. Quoted in Cohen, op. cit., p. 116.
4. See Norberto Bobbio, 'Notta sulla dialectica in Gramsci', in *Studi Gramsciani*.
5. Letter to J. Bloch, quoted in Gustav Mayer *Friedrich Engels, eine Biographie* (The Hague, 1934), vol II, p. 449. See also Gwyn A. Williams, 'Gramsci's concept of *Egemonia*', *Journal of the History of Ideas*, vol. XXI, No. 4, (1960).
6. V. I. Lenin, *Left-Wing Communism, an Infantile Disorder* (Peking, 1970) p. 50.

9. INTELLECTUALS; MACHIAVELLI; 'HEGEMONY'

1. To Tatiana, 15 February 1932, *Lettere del Carcere*. Translated by Hamish Henderson, *The New Edinburgh Review*, 'Gramsci II' (1975) pp. 10-11.

2. To Tatiana, 7 March 1932, *Lettere del Carcere* p. 584. Trans. op. cit., pp. 12-13.
3. ibid.
4. B. Croce, *Materialismo Storico ed Economia Marxistica* (Bari, 1921) p. 112, quoted in *Notes* to *Quaderni del Carcere* p. 2654.

Chronology

1891 Born at Ales in Province of Cagliari, Sardinia. Fourth son of Francesco Gramsci and Giuseppina Marcias.

1903 On completion of elementary education, obliged to leave school and work in local registry office at Ghilarza, where his mother had moved after his father had been imprisoned on charges of maladministration.

1905 Education resumed at secondary schools at Santu Lissurgiu
—1911 and Cagliari.

1911 Awarded scholarship at Turin University and starts studies there.

1913 Witnesses in Sardinia first parliamentary elections on the basis of universal suffrage. Makes first contacts with Italian Socialist Party in Turin.

1914 Begins to contribute articles to Socialist paper *Il Grido del Popolo*. University studies interrupted and then broken off because of ill-health.

1916 Starts to write regularly for Socialist paper *Avanti!*

1917 August. Participates in organization of visit to Turin of delegates from Russian Soviet and increasingly active in Socialist Party.

1919 Co-founder of *L'Ordine Nuovo* and a regular contributor. Active in Turin Factory Councils.

1920 Widespread strikes. September. Participates in occupation of factories.

1921 January. Attends Leghorn (Livorno) congress of Italian Socialist Party, at which party splits and Communist Party is formed. Gramsci becomes member of Central Committee of new party.

1922 June. Arrives in Moscow as member of Executive of Communist International.
      Spends some months in clinic near Moscow, where he meets Giulia Schucht, his future wife.
      October. Fascist 'March on Rome'. Mussolini forms government.

1923 December. Sent by Comintern to Vienna.

1924 April. Elected deputy in Veneto constituency.
      May. Returns to Italy.
      June. Murder of Matteotti. Participates in parliamentary

secession to Aventine but in November Communist deputies decide to return to Chamber and confront Fascists.

1925   March-April. In Moscow for meeting of Comintern executive.
        May. Speaks in Chamber against law banning secret associations.

1926   January. Attends and speaks at national congress of Italian Communist Party at Lyons (France).
        8 November. Arrested in Rome.
        December. Sent to camp for political prisoners at Ustica.

1927   January. Transferred to prison in Milan.

1928   Brought to trial in Rome.
        June. Condemned to twenty years' imprisonment. Sent to Special Penal Establishment at Turi (Bari).

1929   Begins making notes in first Prison Notebook.

1931   August. Suffers serious haemorrhage.

1933   March. Further serious illness. After medical examinations and international campaign transferred (December) to private clinic in Formia.

1935   August. Transferred to Quisisana clinic in Rome.

1937   27 April. Dies after cerebral haemorrhage.

Select Bibliography

1. ITALIAN EDITIONS OF GRAMSCI'S WORKS

(a) The first edition of Gramsci's *Quaderni del Carcere* was published by Einaudi of Turin in six volumes:
   (i) *Il Materialismo Storico e la Filosofia di Benedetto Croce* (1948)
   (ii) *Gli Intellectuali e l'Organizzazione della Cultura* (1949)
   (iii) *Il Risorgimento* (1949)
   (iv) *Note sul Machiavelli, sulla Politica e sullo Stato Moderno* (1949)
   (v) *Letteratura e Vita Nazionale* (1950)
   (vi) *Passato e Presente* (1951)
These have now largely been superseded by the scholarly critical edition in four volumes published under the auspices of the Istituto Antonio Gramsci: *Quaderni del Carcere* a cura di Valentino Gerratana (Torino, Einaudi, 1975).

(b) Gramsci's articles and other writings prior to his imprisonment have been published as follows:
   Scritti Giovanili (1914-18) (Torino, Einaudi, 1958)
   L'Ordine Nuovo (1919-20) (Torino, Einaudi, 1954)
   Sotto la Mole (1916-20) (Torino, Einaudi, 1960)
   Socialismo e Fascismo: L'Ordine Nuovo (1921-22) (Torino, Einaudi, 1967)
   La Costruzione del Partito Comunista (1923-26) (Torino, Einaudi, 1971)

(c) *Lettere del Carcere* a cura di Sergio Caprioglio e Elsa Fubini (Torino, Einaudi, 1965)
   Some unpublished earlier letters, a selection of articles and *Alcuni temi della questione meridionale* are printed in 2000 *Pagine di Gramsci* a cura di Giansiro Ferrata e Niccolo Gallo, of which two of the four projected volumes have been published: Vol. I *Nel tempo della lotta* (1914-26); Vol. II *Lettere edlite e inedite* (1912-37) (Milano, Il Saggiatore, 1964; 1971).

2. ENGLISH TRANSLATIONS OF GRAMSCI'S WORKS

Selections from the Prison Notebooks edited and translated by

Quintin Hoare and Geoffrey Nowell Smith (London, Lawrence and Wishart. New York, International Publishers, 1971)

Letters from Prison selected, translated and introduced by Lynne Lawner. (New York, Harper and Row, 1973. London, Jonathan Cape, 1975)

The New Edinburgh Review, 3 Special Gramsci Numbers, 1974 (edited by C. K. Maisels) contains a translation of a wider selection of the Prison Letters and of other writings.

History, Philosophy and Culture in the Young Gramsci edited by Pedro Cavalanti and Paul Picchon (Saint Louis, Telos Press, 1975) contains a selection of articles from 1914-18.

3. THE FOLLOWING ARE SOME OF THE BOOKS AND ARTICLES ON GRAMSCI AVAILABLE IN ENGLISH:

(a) BOOKS

John M. Cammett, *Antonio Gramsci and the Origins of Italian Communism* (Stanford University Press, 1967)

M. N. Clark, Antonio Gramsci and the Revolution that Failed (London and New York, University of Yale Press, 1977)

A. B. Davidson, *Antonio Gramsci: towards an Intellectual Biography* (London, Merlin Press; Atlantic Highlands, N.J., Humanities Press, 1977)

Giuseppe Fiori, *Antonio Gramsci, Life of a Revolutionary* (London, New Left Books, 1970; New York, Dutton, 1971)

A. Pozzolini, *Antonio Gramsci: an introduction to his thought* (London, Pluto Press, 1970)

Gwyn A. Williams, *Proletarian Order: Antonio Gramsci, Factory Councils and the Origins of Communism in Italy* (London, Pluto Press, 1975)

(b) ARTICLES

Gwyn A. Williams, 'The Concept of Egemonia in the Thought of Antonio Gramsci', *Journal of the History of Ideas*, XXI, 1960

John Merrington, 'Theory and Practice in Gramsci's Marxism', *Socialist Register*, 1968

G. F. Mancini and G. Galli, 'Gramsci's Presence', *Government and Opposition*, III, 1968

V. G. Kiernan, 'Gramsci and Marxism', *Socialist Register*, 1972.

A. B. Davidson, 'The varying seasons of Gramsci studies' *Political Studies*, XX, 1972

Gramsci

E. J. Hobsbawm, 'The Great Gramsci', *New York Review of Books*, XXI, 4 April 1974

Martin Clark, 'The Patron Saint of the Left', *Times Literary Supplement*, 31 October 1975

Thomas R. Bates, 'Gramsci and the Theory of Hegemony', *Journal of the History of Ideas*, XXXVI, 1975

Joseph Femia, 'Hegemony and Consciousness in the Thought of Antonio Gramsci', *Political Studies*, XXIII, 1975.